Fundamentals of
Technical Services Management

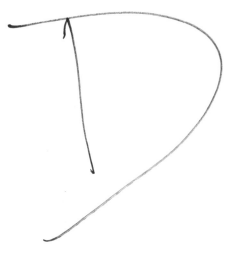

ALA FUNDAMENTALS SERIES

Fundamentals of Children's Services, by Michael Sullivan
Fundamentals of Library Supervision, by Joan Giesecke and
   Beth McNeil

Fundamentals of
TECHNICAL SERVICES MANAGEMENT

SHEILA S. INTNER,
WITH PEGGY JOHNSON

AMERICAN LIBRARY ASSOCIATION   CHICAGO   2008

While extensive effort has gone into ensuring the reliability of information appearing in this book, the publisher makes no warranty, express or implied, on the accuracy or reliability of the information, and does not assume and hereby disclaims any liability to any person for any loss or damage caused by errors or omissions in this publication.

The paper used in this publication meets the minimum requirements of American National Standard for Information Sciences—Permanence of Paper for Printed Library Materials, ANSI Z39.48-1992. ∞

Library of Congress Cataloging-in-Publication Data

Intner, Sheila S.
  Fundamentals of technical services management / Sheila S. Intner, with Peggy Johnson.
    p.   cm. — (ALA fundamentals series)
    Includes bibliographical references and index.
    ISBN 978-0-8389-0953-9 (alk. paper)
    1.   Technical   services   (Libraries)—Management.
  I. Johnson, Peggy, 1948– II. Title.
    Z688.5.I575 2008
    025'.02—dc22   2007030708

ISBN-13: 978-0-8389-0953-9
ISBN-10: 0-8389-0953-1

Printed in the United States of America

12   11   10   09   08   5   4   3   2   1

CONTENTS

v

PREFACE

This book is intended to be a practical manual for managing a technical services department and can also serve as a textbook for course work in this area. Although it is not very long, it covers a variety of essential topics, including the following:

- Styles of administrative organization for technical services functions
- The impact of size on specialization
- Responsibilities of the technical services manager
- Planning technical services policies and programs
- Interacting with vendors, including negotiating contracts and evaluating vendor performance
- Recruiting, training, directing, and supervising staff members, including building teams versus retaining more traditional hierarchies
- Budgeting and overseeing department finances
- The impact of digital resources, including building local digital libraries and participating in cooperative projects
- Interacting within the library community and with those outside the library
- Evaluating department functions and output

The main audience for *Fundamentals of Technical Services Management* is new department managers and assistant managers seeking help with their new duties. The book aims to describe typical issues, problems, and situations encountered in managing a library's technical services department and to suggest solutions and methods of dealing with them. It is also intended for students and faculty doing course work in technical services who are interested in surveying and understanding the activities involved in that area. Practicing technical services librarians who want to become managers can read the book to get an objective view of this important leadership role, and library administrators to whom department managers report can match the book's descriptions against their experiences on the ground. It might even be of assistance to veteran department managers interested in exploring matters with which they are familiar from the authors' point of view.

This book combines the work and thinking of two experienced librarians. Sheila Intner is an educator who has been teaching technical services for more than twenty-five years. Before teaching full-time, she spent seven years practicing in a public library, first as a clerk in technical services; next as a cataloger; then as head of the music department, where she was responsible for cataloging nonprint media; and, last, as coordinator of the library's computer system. Peggy Johnson began her career as a music cataloger and later became a collections specialist. Now she is a senior administrator for a major university research library system. She also teaches students and librarians in both formal and informal venues. Both authors served as president of the Association for Library Collections and Technical Services, the American Library Association division for technical services. Both are or have been editors of scholarly and popular journals. Both have worked, written, consulted, and taught in the United States and around the world about technical services management. They share a vision of the future in which well-managed technical services departments are recognized as the valuable assets they are to their libraries, contributing in direct and visible ways to patron service and the satisfaction of people's information needs.

CHAPTER 1

Administrative Organization of the Department

✧ Introduction and Background
✧ What Is under the Technical Services Umbrella?
✧ Alternative Styles of Organization
✧ Impact of Size
✧ Summary

Introduction and Background

Throughout the nineteenth and twentieth centuries, libraries were organized like government bureaucracies, with three, four, or more levels between the top-level administrators and the line workers at the bottom. Organization charts in the years before automation was introduced typically showed three groups—administrators, technical services workers, and public service workers—linked in a complicated treelike structure. A small number of senior administrators were at the top, supervising junior administrators or department heads who, themselves, supervised department or unit heads who, in turn, supervised line workers. Often, the line workers supervised paraprofessional or nonprofessional staff members serving at the lowest levels in the hierarchy.

Toward the end of the century, however, it became clear that the introduction of computers into libraries was disrupting traditional organization charts by creating new tasks and changing old ones, making some tasks redundant and others obsolete. Work that once was considered professional began filtering down the line to paraprofessionals and nonprofessionals, while middle-management job descriptions began to be upgraded, involving the kinds of risky decision making associated with strategic planning that was once the exclusive province of top management. Eventually, librarians responded by flattening library organization charts. Some institutions went so far as to create self-governing working groups organized around subject areas, with no supervisory links between administrators and line workers. Others eliminated a few, but not all, of the bureaucratic layers by reorganizing tasks and changing procedures to streamline their operations.

Early computerization was mainly aimed at bibliographic files—catalogs, order files, serials control files, circulation control files—most located in the technical services department. As computers took over the work of order clerks, typists, filers, alphabetizers, and others, the need to rethink and revise procedures became critical. At the same time, networking and data sharing enabled basic bibliographic tasks such as cataloging to be performed more efficiently and at lower cost by nonlibrary specialists, which contributed further to the disruption and prompted more change. Three words dominated technical services literature and terrorized its workers: reorganization, downsizing, and outsourcing. In the last decade of the twentieth century, a major shift took place in technical services staffing. Quite a few senior staff retired to avoid the trauma of reorganization or the possibility they would have to learn new jobs; some were reassigned either voluntarily or involuntarily; and a few, who found themselves unable to function in the new library organization, resigned. Replacements tended to have different skills, different job descriptions, and a different set of expectations for their work.

After automating, the new technical services department was, indeed, leaner. In some places, the specialties of acquisitions, cataloging, and inventory control were combined with public service activities, creating broad-based, self-governing, subject-oriented groups that took advantage of subject expertise rather than functional expertise. In such units, catalogers learned to answer reference questions, teach patrons how to retrieve information, and oversee the computer systems through which materials were obtained and tracked while in use. Reference librarians learned to catalog and track materials as well as to answer questions, teach, and select titles for purchase. In other places, cataloging was outsourced to a cooperative group or a commercial organization, usually in an effort to minimize the need for high-priced, in-house cataloging experts and deploy existing staff more effectively. A few of these libraries later revived their cataloging units but in streamlined forms.

What Is under the Technical Services Umbrella?

Technical services units, past and present, cover some or all of the following functions: (1) acquiring books and monographic titles in other formats (e.g., musical scores, videos, and visual images), usually by purchasing them but sometimes

In *Budgeting for Information Access,* authors Murray S. Martin and Milton T. Wolf use the categories below to analyze acquisitions methods for budget purposes. The same approach is useful for organizing an acquisitions unit.

A. Direct purchase
  Publisher
  Dealer
  Agent
B. Approval plans and blanket orders
C. Subscriptions
  Direct
  Vendor
D. Standing orders
  Publisher
  Vendor
E. Gift and exchange
  Books [and monographs in other media]
  Periodicals

Source: Murray S. Martin and Milton T. Wolf, *Budgeting for Information Access: Managing the Resource Budget for Absolute Access* (Chicago: American Library Association, 1998), 99.

also by leasing access to them; (2) cataloging and processing these materials; (3) acquiring, cataloging, and maintaining inventory control over periodicals and other serially issued publications; and (4) preserving locally held materials, including binding, reformatting, repairing, and managing their storage. Since the advent of computerized bibliographic data, supervision of circulation control has been added to the list, although in precomputer days that function was almost always subsumed under the public services umbrella.

Changes prompted by computers include combining the acquisition and cataloging functions, especially for monographic titles (the result of finding standard bibliographic records for them during preorder searches); shifting from original to copy cataloging for most titles; processing materials differently to accommodate and take advantage of computer-readable labels and the like; and, perhaps most important of all, tracking materials automatically, whether they are moving through initial processing, being sent temporarily to a binder or a conservation lab, or being borrowed by patrons.

In some libraries, the name of the department has changed to reflect the changes in the way work is accomplished, usually incorporating words and phrases such as *automation, computer, bibliographic control,* or *database services.* Generally, technical services departments, whatever they are called, are still the locus for these activities, provided they are done in-house and have not been outsourced, but there are other methods of organizing them.

Alternative Styles of Organization

The functions that are typically under the aegis of a technical services group are often associated with behind-the-scenes work or work based on a library's own bibliographic files, but there are other approaches to organizing such activities. Four alternatives are (1) placing serials and binding under reference/information services; (2) maintaining a separate computer or bibliographic services department to handle all database work, including contracting for electronic resources, entering and maintaining catalog records, and the like; (3) establishing a separate, free-standing preservation department, with or without assigning bindery work to it; and (4) expanding circulation services into an access services unit that includes interlibrary loans and document delivery, subsumed under the library's public services group.

Placing Serials under a Reference/Information Services Group

Scholarly journals and other periodicals tend to be collected in larger numbers by libraries that have a substantial research mission than by libraries for which research support plays a smaller role. For the most part, libraries in colleges and universities are strongly research oriented, although numerous public library collections support research and, in this respect, resemble their academic counterparts. In these libraries, periodicals may be designated "reference" and do not circulate. Before reference materials were computerized, the idea was to locate periodicals close to the indexes to their contents, which were located in the reference department. When periodicals are subsumed under reference, all the activities associated with them—even activities typically assigned to technical services—are done by members of the reference staff, including acquisitions, cataloging, inventory, circulation control, binding, and collection maintenance.

The advantages of putting periodicals under reference are (1) their proximity to indexes and other associated reference tools, (2) their storage with other noncirculating materials, and (3) their proximity to librarians ready to help patrons find needed information in them. The disadvantages of putting periodicals under reference are (1) having to train reference staff to perform the tasks of acquiring, cataloging, and processing periodicals instead of using technical services staff, who already are expert in such work; (2) preparing and maintaining separate bibliographic files for periodicals; and (3) fragmenting subject-oriented materials in different locations based on publication patterns (periodical versus monographic), not on content.

Maintaining a Separate Computer Services Department

In the early days of automation (that is, in the 1960s and 1970s), some libraries concentrated all their computer-related activities in one department, separate from the existing departments. Two reasons seemed to dictate the logic of this organizational style: (1) hardware (which then meant large mainframe computers or minicomputers that required a strictly controlled environment to function properly) was accommodated in a defined location that also could be secured easily; and (2) staff with computer expertise (which, in those days, often meant the ability to write programs) were housed together as a group. Once the tradition was established, it may have seemed harder to change than to continue, even when networked microcomputers made distributed processing a more effective way of organizing computer services.

Libraries that built new wings or redid sections of their existing space to provide the electrical wiring, outlets, and other physical infrastructure needed for computers, as well as the ergonomic furnishings favored by computer specialists, likely found it more agreeable and less costly to move increased numbers of staff using computers, such as cataloging data entry staff, into the new or improved space than to rewire and refurbish the rest of the library. The idea that every staff member needs a computer to function is a recent one. It emerged with the advent of the Internet, which, at this writing, is less than two decades old—not old enough to have superseded established tradition.

The advantages of maintaining a separate computer services department include (1) minimizing the amount of physical improvement a library had to undertake; (2) keeping hardware in a defined area that could be secured easily; (3) locating staff with computer expertise together; and (4) combining tasks from departments reporting to different groups in the library, such as cataloging and circulation, that require similar kinds of data entry and ongoing database maintenance. With the passage of time and the current need for nearly all staff to use computers to do their work, some of these advantages have lost value. The disadvantages of maintaining a separate computer services department include (1) creating unnecessary barriers between computer staff and staff of other library departments; (2) preventing computer staff from sharing their knowledge easily, on an informal, ongoing, day-to-day basis with other library staff who need at least some of this knowledge; and (3) creating artificial boundaries between library work in general and library work done through computers. These disadvantages, if allowed to continue unchecked, could decrease overall efficiency in the long run.

Establishing a Free-Standing Preservation Department

Preservation activities are often centered in the technical services department because they relate, to some degree, to processing and binding tasks. Binding and rebinding are among the principal preservation strategies used to extend the life of books, periodicals, and other paper-based materials. In many small and medium-sized libraries, preservation as an extension of binding and other physical treatments for materials is performed in a small, though important, collection management unit, best administered within the larger department. If a project arises that requires more resources than the unit has available, it can be outsourced to a specialized organization such as the Northeast Document Conservation Center (NEDCC), or the library can assemble a temporary team of consultants to complete it.

In very large libraries with massive numbers of items needing to be treated, however, it makes sense to have a separate, free-standing department whose agenda goes beyond binding loose issues of periodicals or adding plastic covers and inserting security strips into new books. In these libraries, there is more than enough work to be done to keep a well-staffed department humming. Such a department might include a conservation laboratory as well as an ordinary repair unit, an education unit, a survey unit, a disaster response team, a reformatting laboratory, and other specialized units dealing with individual types of materials, such as films, magnetic tape recordings, maps, manuscripts, and visual images. Directed by a knowledgeable preservationist, the stand-alone department can customize its activities to fit the problems of local collections and follow local policies and priorities.

The advantages of having a separate preservation department are (1) acquiring sufficient budget and space to house the staff, equipment,

Types of damage to books that can be treated by in-house processing and repair units:

- Dirt and markings, excluding markings made with indelible inks
- Torn pages
- Detached pages
- Loose hinges
- Torn endpapers
- Partly detached covers (which usually have torn endpapers)
- Detached spines, especially the caps
- Detached cases/text blocks

Common repairs that can extend the life of books not valuable as artifacts:*

- Cleaning covers and pages
- Repairing pages
- Tipping in loose or replacement pages
- Tightening hinges
- Replacing endpapers
- Repairing or replacing spines
- Recasing with original or replacement boards

Source: Adapted from *Gaylord Preservation Pathfinder No. 4: An Introduction to Book Repair* (Syracuse, NY: Gaylord Bros., 1995), 3.

* If a book has artifactual value, it should not be repaired or treated by anyone other than a trained conservator. Ordinary repairs can destroy the value of the object, even though they might make it look better from a layperson's point of view. Imagine, for example, that a library is bequeathed a mid-nineteenth-century book that has margin notes handwritten by President Abraham Lincoln. If the notes are erased to make the book clean, the Lincoln notes, which would have made the book extremely valuable, will be lost.

and supplies needed to do a wide range of repair and conservation work within the library; (2) facilitating interaction among specialized staff members, some of whom may not be librarians; (3) raising the organizational status of the preservation department head to the same level as that of the technical services department head, thus freeing preservation from a subordinate position; and (4) creating a department that can customize its work to fit the needs of the local library. The disadvantages of having a separate preservation department are (1) isolating specialists from others who could benefit from their knowledge, such as those doing the routine processing of materials; (2) adding another department to the library that must be funded, staffed, supervised, and evaluated; and (3) spending more money to do preservation tasks in-house than to outsource them with equal or better results.

Expanding Circulation into an Access Services Unit

As computerized networking matured, it became easier and almost instantaneous for librarians in one library to find out where desired, but internally unavailable, titles were held as well as to send requests for these titles to the holding libraries. Interlibrary loans jumped from modest numbers of transactions to a total of twelve million or more a year for members of the Online Computer Library Center (OCLC) bibliographic network system. At the same time, commercial suppliers of documents—generally articles from journals—became increasingly able to provide desired material through the Internet. As the several routes used by patrons to obtain desired materials developed—that is, borrowing from local collections, borrowing from other libraries, and buying from outside sources—it seemed logical to place them all within one unit, where they could be handled by staff familiar with the transactions and the computer systems they employed. Instead of handling only local circulation, the enhanced access services unit handled the transfer of documents to patrons no matter where the materials originated.

Not all units named "access services" hold authority over circulation, interlibrary loan, and document delivery. Some libraries limited

When access services includes circulation, the manager can have surprising adventures. The head of access services at an Ivy League university recalled such an adventure caused by a faculty member who abused his privileges for years by borrowing books in large numbers but not returning them. The manager tried every strategy she could think of to recover the books, including personally calling at his residence accompanied by campus security guards, but nothing succeeded. One day she was summoned by the police to an apartment in a building near the campus. The faculty member, who had by then retired, had rented the apartment to use as an office after vacating his departmental office. Neighbors, who suspected that something had happened to the man, had called the police. They were correct. The police arrived on the scene and had to break down the door. Stepping inside, they found the unfortunate faculty member's body and concluded that he had suffered a fatal heart attack and died in the midst of the collection of books. Instead of buying office furnishings, the man had simply filled the apartment with books he had borrowed from the university library. Based on the markings in the books, the police knew whom to call to return the collection to its rightful owner.

the expansion of circulation services to control over physical access to collections, authorizing them to determine who could enter the library and use the materials, borrow them, or use them within the library. Several member organizations of the Association of Research Libraries limited access to their immediate service population (that is, holders of valid institutional identification cards) for several reasons: they lacked sufficient staff to monitor and track the use of valuable or fragile materials, a few had been victims of theft and vandalism, and it was clear that lost or damaged items were not replaceable. The job of deciding who could have access to library materials was assigned to the access services unit along with the former duties of the circulation department, including checking materials in and out, shelving returned materials, and carrying out policies for materials that were overdue, damaged, or lost while in the possession of a patron. In this or the previously described situation, the circulation department took on new duties and added importance, which sometimes justified its designation as a stand-alone unit.

The advantages of an expanded access services department include (1) combining related tasks, whether these are providing wanted materials no matter what their source or monitoring access to and use of local materials; (2) raising the status of the work, which, to patrons, is of great importance; and (3) focusing the training and expertise with the associated computer systems among a well-defined group of staff members. The disadvantages of an expanded access services department are (1) broadening already stressful jobs by adding more potentially unpleasant tasks, such as denying access to people who are not eligible to use the library or dealing with patrons who want their interlibrary loans to arrive more quickly; (2) having to train members of the new group, including some who may be the least prepared, to implement complex policies and use sophisticated computer systems in doing so; and (3) combining tasks that, possibly, are not as closely related as they appear on the surface.

Impact of Size

It seems logical that the larger an organization is, the more likely it is that related types of work will develop into specialties, simply because of the larger volume of every type of activity, from ordering materials and cataloging them to answering patrons' questions and obtaining interlibrary loans.[1] Benefits of specialization can be realized, up to a point, by concentrating related tasks into units whose staff deal only with that kind of work. However, something is lost as well, primarily the flexibility that comes with having many employees who can do a variety of jobs and the diversity of tasks that can make a job more interesting.

Librarians have long debated whether libraries should seek employees who are specialists or generalists. Observers can find evidence of greater effectiveness from both kinds of people, depending on the time, the place, and the situation as well as the individuals involved. For instance, librarians working in very small libraries rarely can allow themselves the luxury of specializing in what they like to do best. Directors of small libraries must pitch in and do what needs to be done, whether it is checking in and shelving a stack of returned books, cataloging a box of new DVDs, or presenting next year's budget to a town board. Some librarians in large libraries believe they can achieve better morale and higher productivity when specialization is de-emphasized and preparation and training in running a variety of library systems is universal or nearly so. Job descriptions that mandate part-time work in technical services and part-time work in public services (known as dual-role positions) have been offered and accepted willingly by new hires.

Library size, while an important factor in deciding how best to organize tasks, does not always demand the same response. Instead, a range of organizational responses can be considered that take into account the number and knowledge of existing staff members, the service priorities of the library, the library's technical infrastructure and level of readiness for one or another method of organization, and the comfort level of the key players with more or less specialization and hierarchy in the library's administrative structure.

Summary

The functions almost always included under the technical services umbrella, regardless of what the department is called, are acquisitions, cataloging, and processing. Two of the three functions can be interpreted broadly or narrowly. Cataloging almost always covers both original and copy cataloging, although, in some libraries, so little original cataloging is done that the operation is almost all copy work. But acquisitions might cover both monographs and serially published titles or only monographs. If serials are excluded, a separate serials control unit might be included under technical services, reference/public services, or as a stand-alone department. Processing might cover the initial processing of new materials and the reprocessing, binding, and repair of old materials as well as specialized preservation services, or it might include only the initial processing of new materials. If it covers only the initial processing of new materials, one or more separate units covering the other services could be subsumed under technical services or public services, or organized as stand-alone departments. Circulation control, interlibrary loan, and document delivery might or might not be added to the three basic functions of technical services, however these are interpreted, or they might be organized under reference/public services or as stand-alone departments.

The nature of administrative organization in any one library, information center, learning center, or media center depends on a combination of factors, mainly its tradition, its environment, and the ideas of its leaders. When interpreted broadly, the technical services department is likely to be large and busy, handling many different types of tasks. To the extent that functions eligible to be administered under technical services are placed under reference/public services or are separate departments, technical services will be smaller and more focused. No one method of organization is best, nor will a good method remain good for all time. It behooves administrators to be open-minded about adopting different organizational styles in order to improve their bibliographical outputs and the working environment.

Recommended Reading

Evans, G. Edward, Sheila S. Intner, and Jean Weihs. *Introduction to Technical Services.* 7th ed. Westport, CT: Libraries Unlimited, 2002.

Godden, Irene P., ed. *Library Technical Services: Operations and Management.* 2nd ed. San Diego: Academic Press, 1991.

Gorman, Michael, et al. *Technical Services, Today and Tomorrow.* 2nd ed. Englewood, CO: Libraries Unlimited, 1998.

Intner, Sheila S. "A Giant Step Backward for Technical Services," *Library Journal* 110, no. 7 (April 15, 1985): 43–45. [Discusses the impact of library size on technical services departments.]

Intner, Sheila S., and Josephine Riss Fang. *Technical Services in the Medium-Sized Library: An Investigation of Current Practices.* Hamden, CT: Library Professional Publications, 1991.

Tauber, Maurice, et al. *Technical Services in Libraries.* New York: Columbia University Press, 1954. [The first and still the landmark work describing technical services functions and their management; it has never been equaled.]

Note

1. The issue of size is discussed in detail in Sheila S. Intner's "A Giant Step Backward for Technical Services," *Library Journal* 110, no. 7 (April 15, 1985): 43–45.

CHAPTER 2

Responsibilities and Authority of the Manager

- ✧ Planning and Directing Operations
- ✧ Staffing and Staff Supervision
- ✧ Managing Technology
- ✧ Managing the Departmental Budget
- ✧ Evaluating Departmental Outputs
- ✧ Beyond Departmental Borders
- ✧ Summary

THE RESPONSIBILITIES of the technical services manager sound like those of all managers: planning and directing the department's operations; supervising its staff members; managing its budget; evaluating departmental outputs; and representing the department beyond its borders, within and outside of the library, to peers in other libraries, to library vendors, to patrons, and to the rest of the outside world. Depending on the size of the library, the number of specialized departmental units, and the level of activity in its technical services operations, a department manager might be the sole supervisor (generally true for small libraries in which there are no specialized units) or might share supervisory duties with an assistant or with several assistant managers (for example, one for each unit—a likely scenario in large libraries in which there are many specialized units and many staff members), delegating limited powers to them. A single assistant manager is likely to be given authority to supervise a particular task, such as personnel management or dealing with suppliers and other external vendors. Unit heads are likely to have authority for supervising the work within their units, but it might or might not include all areas of responsibility. For example, the department manager might retain authority over decisions affecting the budget, involving the interpretation of library policy, or dealing with major personnel matters.

The technical services manager's most important responsibilities, whether or not he or she delegates any part of the managerial authority to another, are ensuring that library policies are properly interpreted and implemented, that the workload is fairly distributed, and that all the work that is supposed to be done is done well and in a timely and cost-effective manner. The manager's desk is where the buck stops. When things go right, a wise manager allows his or her assistants, unit heads, and other subordinates to take the credit. When things go wrong, a good manager shoulders the blame, even if it actually belongs to someone else to whom authority over the problem area was delegated.

Planning and Directing Operations

Library Policies

Determining work flow—what gets done, in what order, using which procedures and technology, and producing which specific products—is a major part of planning and directing operations, but a new manager should not begin there. The policies of the library concerning all technical service functions (acquiring materials, cataloging and processing them, using and preserving them, and so forth) should guide the manager's decisions about work-flow design. In order to be sure they are understood, the department manager should make sure that the policies are written in clear language and that all employees, new and veteran, know what they are. If a library has no existing policies, the manager needs to create them, preferably using a collaborative process so that people at all levels, including library patrons, have a chance to contribute, react, and understand what decisions are made and why. In addition, the department's priorities, which must be consistent with library-wide priorities, need to be understood and accepted.

D iscovering problems and improving operations is not easy. One approach is for managers to ask what happens to data or materials as they travel through technical services from start to finish. Useful questions include the following:

1. With regard to efficiency:
   - Is the work flow uniform and, if not, are plans in place to accommodate peaks and valleys?
   - Is any procedure repeated or any information duplicated?
   - Is material transported over a distance of more than a few yards?
   - Does material or information ever backtrack?
   - Do work backlogs occur at any point?
   - Can the result of any procedure be obtained faster? With less work? By redeploying staff? By outsourcing?
   - How does patron service benefit from the procedure?
   - What would happen if the procedure were eliminated?
2. With regard to quality:
   - Do errors occur and, if so, what kinds, how many, when, and why?
   - Do these errors prevent patrons from obtaining needed information or materials?
   - Can errors be eliminated through staff training? By adding product reviews? By changing methods? By adopting different tools or equipment? By outsourcing?
3. With regard to cost:
   - Can less costly staff be trained to do a particular task without eroding quality?
   - Can products of equal or better quality be purchased from an outside source at lower cost?
   - Can productivity be increased through training, instituting new methods, or adopting new tools or equipment or both?

Department Priorities

Policies tend to be written without regard to their relative importance. In a way, all of them are equally important; however, sometimes following them all requires more resources than a library has at its disposal. In these instances, an individual library's priorities dictate which policies to follow. For example, if library policies are to obtain materials as quickly as possible and also to buy materials at the best prices, it is difficult to follow both simultaneously. A choice usually must be made between speed and cost.

A policy that should have the highest priority for every technical services department is that it should complete all of its work within a reasonable time frame. *Reasonable* can be defined subjectively, but completing the year's work within two to three weeks, or a month, at most, beyond the year's end seems appropriate. Permitting repeated shortfalls in the work flow to build is disastrous because, sooner or later, it turns into a crisis. Completing all the work within a limited time frame sometimes means accepting less-than-perfect products in order to speed operations, such as creating minimal-level cataloging for selected categories of materials cataloged in-house and restricting the amount of editing done to source records before copying them into the local catalog. Striving for perfect products can cause the department to fall so far behind that it becomes impossible to catch up without a large infusion of extra resources—resources that are hard to obtain.

Goals and Objectives

Department goals and objectives should be derived from the policies and be put in writing so that everyone knows what work is supposed to be accomplished. Goals tend to describe intended outcomes in general terms. Objectives provide the details and strategies for accomplishing them and need to be written in specific, measurable terms. The objectives will later provide the means for evaluating the department's work, discussed in greater detail in chapter 9. For example, a departmental goal for processing might be to protect materials from damage. Objectives serving this goal could include strategies such as using archival-quality

Writing measurable objectives requires a kind of creativity that is rarely taught in academic programs. Still, library managers have to define what they want to accomplish in specific terms. Imagine this scenario: public services staff report to the library director that books in the youth paperback fiction collection are being damaged after one or two uses and must be replaced. The director calls in the technical services manager and asks her to take measures to increase the shelf life of such books. The manager, in turn, must translate the goal of increasing shelf life into objectives that, if accomplished, will do the job.

The manager consults with the processing and preservation staff and learns that damage can be prevented as well as repaired. Strengthening the books prevents damage from occurring, and instituting a repair program gets damaged books back in circulation and avoids having to order replacement copies. To make the objectives of strengthening new books and repairing damaged books measurable, number-based targets are added, even if the numbers are hidden. For example:

In processing new youth paperback fiction:

Laminate the covers of all copies. (A number is hidden in the word *all*—if the library buys one hundred books, one hundred covers must be laminated before the books are shelved.)

Reinforce the spines of series titles identified as the most likely to get heavy use. (In this case, the number is hidden in the phrase "series titles identified as the most likely to get heavy use." The youth librarian can identify such series, and all books purchased that are part of those series must have their spines reinforced as well as their covers laminated.)

(continued on page 20)

Hire a part-time processing unit staff member to handle these tasks.

Immediately estimate and purchase needed supplies and equipment.

In treating preexisting copies of youth paperback fiction:

Designate one processing unit staff member responsible for repairs of youth paperback fiction. (This assignment may be temporary.)

Within two weeks, train the designated staff member in common repairs: torn covers, torn pages, broken text blocks.

Raise the priority level for repair of youth paperback fiction to ensure a three-day turnaround.

Laminate the covers of all repaired books.

Reinforce the spines of all repaired books that are part of the identified heavily used series.

Laminate the covers of all undamaged youth paperback fiction books.

Reinforce the spines of all undamaged youth paperback fiction titles that are part of the identified heavily used series.

Immediately estimate and purchase supplies and equipment needed.

The technical services manager estimates the amount of work to be done and the staff hours required as well as the needed supplies and equipment. It could take more than one full-time staff member to satisfy the three-day turnaround time, depending on the number of books to be treated and the types of repairs they need. Once all the damaged books and existing undamaged books are treated, the flow of work will diminish; thus, the position designated for repair can be temporary. On the other hand, the added processing for new books and some repairs will continue to be done, so the part-time position designated for new processing is likely to be permanent.

ownership labels, binding new paperback books before shelving them, and using heavy-duty carrying cases for DVDs.

Procedures

Once objectives have been written that clarify what work is to be done, procedures for accomplishing the work can be developed. For example, an objective stating that archival-quality ownership labels will be used informs staff members that they are to use ownership labels, not stamps, embossers, or other types of ownership devices, and that the labels must meet archival-quality standards.

A technical services department that has several units handling many functions needs to develop procedures for each function. In fact, there must be procedures for each work flow within a function. This development process is not a one-time-only effort; it needs to be ongoing. Department managers can choose to lead the development process themselves or delegate parts or all of it to assistants or unit heads. For example, ongoing review and development of cataloging procedures might be delegated to the head of the cataloging unit, processing procedures to the head of the processing unit, and so on.

Most new department managers will not need to design procedures from scratch. Instead, they will inherit procedures established by their predecessors, and attempts to revise them may make it seem as though they are fiddling with tradition. Once routines are established and staff members are trained in doing them, change is neither simple nor easy. But even veteran managers who have thought through the way jobs are done very carefully and settled on procedures should revisit each operation on a regular basis, even when it seems to be working smoothly, asking whether changes are warranted. If this is done regularly instead of in response to a crisis, changes can become part of the normal routine and, therefore, more tolerable, especially if stress factors such as temporarily lower outputs are accepted and rewards given for adopting the changes.

Keeping track of all the procedures is not a simple job, but it is important and should not be left to chance. Procedures need to be put in writing, both as a method of training (and retraining) staff members and as a way of ensuring consistent outputs.[1] Procedures must be reviewed regularly and changes considered that save time and money or improve the quality and performance of the department's products and services.

Planning the Department's Work Flow

Work-flow planning combines all the necessary procedures into a smooth-functioning operation that proceeds with specific end results in mind. The work flow should reflect the policies and priorities of the department and the library. For example, if cataloging is to be completed within three workdays after receiving materials in the cataloging unit, editing every subfield of source records used in copy cataloging or agonizing for days over the assignment of subject headings and call numbers might not be possible. Managers must figure out how much work is to be done and how many staff hours they have to do it (leaving room for absences due to illness, conferences, snow days, and the like) as well as allotting a little time and money for revision of existing work. Then, doing the math reveals how much time can be spent on individual items or types of items, since different materials may need different kinds of handling. Strategizing about how to streamline procedures and how to distribute the flow of work evenly should also be factored into the equation. Often, in the acquisitions unit, work flow is either feast or famine. That is not a good way to operate. If it is the norm, as it could be for schools that order materials only once a year, work assignments would have to be adjusted to account for times when orders are being processed and times when ordering is completed and different work needs to fill the workday.

Senior staff can be engaged in helping plan the department's work flow. Not only have they earned the right to be consulted and exert some measure of control over how they do their jobs, but also some will be very good at organizing their work. One strategy for obtaining their help is organizing teams consisting of one expert and several assisting staff to plan the work flow for their functional areas.

EVANS'S TIME-MANAGEMENT TIPS

1. When you receive a notice that requires action, avoid time-consuming paper shuffling by immediately completing the specified tasks. Rereading notices takes time that could be saved if actions are taken right away.

2. Whenever possible, complete tasks well before their deadlines. Unforeseen circumstances, such as delays in obtaining needed supplies, equipment, or staff assistance; mislaid instructions; or the need to attend to other important tasks can crop up and increase the stress of meeting your deadline or even prevent you from meeting it.

3. Create to-do lists and arrange them chronologically. For example, for the current week make lists titled "To do Monday," "To do Tuesday," and so on. Then proceed to "To do next week," "To do in 2 weeks," and so forth for the balance of the month.

4. File materials related to the tasks on your to-do lists by their due dates, not by their dates of receipt.

5. Analyze a complex project into a series of component tasks with due dates that fall before the final deadline. This maintains a positive sense of progress and allows time for unexpected or unavoidable delays that might occur along the way.

6. Batch telephone calls and set aside a specific block of time during the workday for making, returning, and receiving calls. Ask colleagues, vendors, and others you work with to call during that time period, and specify when to call back in the voice-mail messages you leave for people you call but do not reach.

7. Spend a few minutes planning the calls you must make. Use a large writing pad to note the information you need to convey or learn during each call and stick to those points when you talk. File your notes with the related tasks or projects.

(continued on page 24)

8. Limit each telephone call to a few minutes. If a call requires more time, consider communicating by e-mail, memorandum, note, or letter.

9. Batch e-mailing tasks and complete them during a designated time that can overlap with your telephone time. For example, set aside 9:30 to 11:00 a.m. for both, first making telephone calls and then e-mailing for the balance of the time. If someone calls after you begin e-mail, you are at your desk and can take the call if you wish. Add a brief time at the end of the day for an e-mail review so that you can read replies to earlier messages and answer important new messages before you leave.

10. Designate a time during the day when staff members and other colleagues are welcome to drop in without an appointment, or, alternatively, establish that unplanned visits are welcome only when your door is open. Set time limits for drop-in visitors and stick to them (for example, say, "I can give you five minutes").

Source: Adapted from G. Edward Evans et al., *Introduction to Technical Services,* 7th ed. (Westport, CT: Libraries Unlimited, 2002), 42–44.

Policy Manuals

Policies can be gathered into a manual and made available to anyone who wishes or needs to see them. The manual might include everything: overall policies, like the classification and subject heading authorities used and bibliographic level followed, as well as current goals, objectives, and procedures, including nitpicky details such as how to treat monographic series or local authors. Or policy manuals might be brief and cover only basic decisions governing the department's work. Policy-only manuals must be supplemented by documents that spell out departmental goals and objectives and the procedures to be used in implementing them.

Thoughtful department managers prepare policy manuals in two formats: online and hard copy. Hard copy is much easier to read, but an online version is important because it is far easier to update. New hard-copy versions can be generated on a regular basis or only after changes have been made to the online versions.

Staffing and Staff Supervision

One responsibility of a department manager is making sure staff members understand what work they have to do and how their work will be evaluated. Assuming that every staff member knows what is expected of him or her is risky, even with regard to individuals who have worked in the library longer than the manager has. Even though department members may be able to tell a newly appointed manager a lot about how things have been done in the past, that is not the same as knowing how this manager wants things done in the future. At the same time, the staff members have a lot to learn about what the manager thinks should be done and how the work should be accomplished.

When a new manager questions staff members about who does what and how they do it, it can be interpreted as an effort to maintain the status quo when that is not true. A new manager needs to understand what is going on in the department before deciding whether changes are warranted and, if so, how to make them. If the new manager is a departmental insider who has been promoted to manager, it can be harder to alter the status quo and establish new routines, but if changes are needed, it must be done. Inquiries should be accompanied by the information that asking how things are done is not endorsing those routines but merely fact finding. Methods of communicating with staff on these subjects (and others) include the following:

Holding meaningful staff meetings regularly and listening to what people say at them. Some good rules to follow about staff meetings are (1) always have an agenda; (2) give advance notice to people you expect to contribute to the meeting—do not spring participation on them with everyone watching; (3) always follow through with anything you promise to do and report back; (4) expect others to do the same and give them a chance to do it.

Being approachable. Try to recognize and address problems before they become crises. Never scold someone for bringing a problem to your attention; instead, thank the person and reward him or her somehow.

Making sure other units of the library know how the department operates and what impacts it might have on their work flow. The bigger the library, the more likely it is that unintended consequences will occur whenever anything new is done, but that does not mean nothing new should happen. It means people have to be aware of what is going on and be ready to address problems in a positive spirit, not with a "what is good for me and forget anyone else" attitude.

Like all department heads, the technical services manager is responsible for recruiting and hiring; training and *retraining* department librarians and other staff members (needed continuously, primarily because the computer systems on which we rely for much of our work are constantly being upgraded); providing professional-development opportunities; assigning and overseeing work and evaluating the work done; evaluating employees and writing recommendations for them as needed; and, last but not least, maintaining morale. Individual institutions have their own hiring methods and processes within which the manager must operate. That said, leading or participating actively in the hiring process is a positive step for the manager to take in ensuring a competent staff. Once new staff members are hired, the manager is responsible for integrating them into the department and overseeing their work as well as continuing to guide and monitor veteran staff members.

Some staff supervision may be delegated to subordinates, especially if the department is large and divided into a number of units. In that

Changes in policy and procedure have unintended consequences. In the mid-1970s, in a suburban public library system consisting of a main library and three branches, each of which
had a card catalog for the materials in the unit, intralibrary loans
among the units were a tiny fraction of circulation. The main library
acquired titles that were not purchased for the branches, but the
branches could not order titles unless copies were also purchased
for the main library. Statistics showed that branch patrons borrowed
overwhelmingly from their local branch, and if they wanted a title
available only at the main library, they went there in person and
borrowed it.

At the close of the decade, the library bought a computerized
circulation system and spent months loading data for patrons and
existing collections. When the new system was ready for public
use, the library director made a small policy change. Because the
computer displayed data for every item in the system regardless
of where it was shelved, he allowed branches to buy titles that the
main library did not own. In the first year, the total of intralibrary
loans jumped from approximately four thousand to sixty-four thousand. Daily, a mountain of materials had to be picked from the
shelves of each unit and taken to other units. While welcoming the
leap in circulation, the main library had to hire more staff to pick
the materials off the shelves, pack them in boxes, and deliver them.
They went from one daily delivery per unit to two on weekdays. The
branches needed more desk staff to handle unpacking, sorting, and
lending more materials. Patrons, however, enjoyed the "new" titles
they found and the greater convenience. Now they did not have to
go to the main library; the main library came to their branch.

event, each unit head may be responsible for on-the-job training, task assignment, work oversight, and part of staff evaluation, such as collecting and reporting production statistics, measuring product quality, and so on. However, the department head is still responsible for signing and submitting the final versions of staff evaluations and writing individual recommendations. Managers are likely to retain direct oversight of staff development, recruiting and hiring new people, and informing existing staff of voluntary or involuntary reassignments.

The manager functions as a communications conduit for the department, informing staff about and explaining new policies and directives made at higher administrative levels as well as taking staff complaints and suggestions up the line to library administrators and making sure they are given serious consideration. The communications role is not neutral because managers often have great latitude in how and when they convey news to their staff and to their superiors. A good manager will work hard to communicate effectively. Doing so not only can pay off in better outputs but also contributes to building morale. People want to feel that they know what is happening in their workplace and that those for whom they work are willing to listen to what they have to say.

Managing Technology

Technology can be a positive tool or a stumbling block in the work of the department. Special attention to the smooth operation of computers and other high-tech systems used by the department is an important responsibility for the manager. Even when the department manager is not a technical expert, smooth-running technical systems are one of his or her responsibilities. Managers must understand their departments' existing systems; know what else is out there in the marketplace that might replace them, what such systems cost, and what they can do; and be ready when asked to make recommendations to the library's top administration.

Responsibility for troubleshooting problems when existing systems break down often falls to the manager in small libraries in which no other staff member has been hired to do it. Finding the causes of problems can be time consuming and requires constant updating of technical knowledge. If troubleshooting consumes so much time that other important tasks fail to get done, department managers need to consider alternatives to doing it themselves and find other solutions. Options include paying for service contracts; hiring a technical consultant and, perhaps, sharing the cost with other departments within the library or with technical services managers in peer libraries having similar problems; or occasionally borrowing a knowledgeable staff member from another department on a temporary basis.

Knowing what is happening in the technology marketplace is also important, just like knowing when new cataloging rules are going to take effect or when a new tool is issued. Technology is more than a tool these days. It is part and parcel of determining what technical services tasks can be performed as well as how they are structured. No manager should have to rely on others to explain what is happening in the world of technology outside the library or what trends could affect the department's work.

Managing the Departmental Budget

The technical services manager may or may not be responsible for setting up the department's budget, but he or she is always responsible for monitoring it during the fiscal year and reporting on what was spent and how it was spent. If possible, a good manager should try to get the authority to set up the budget. Budget power confers real power to control the department's activities, operations, staffing, and more.

Whether or not a manager sets up the budget, he or she must always be aware of how much it costs to produce each type of output. For example, how much does it cost to catalog a video? Process an order? Bind a periodical volume? Obtain something via interlibrary loan? Tighten a loose book spine? Not knowing basic costs hobbles the manager in planning for the department, answering questions and criticism about department activities, and making intelligent, informed decisions about work flow and staffing.

When things are going smoothly, it is easy to be complacent about what is happening. A good manager thinks about experimenting with new modes of operation that could save money without adversely affecting services. And with responsibility for spending money goes responsibility for obtaining it. A good manager thinks about seeking new sources of income when budgets fall short of funding basic services at reasonable quality levels.

Outsourcing is one way libraries have tried to save money on technical services tasks. In some instances it succeeds; in others it fails. It all depends on what is being outsourced, to whom, and at what prices. Outsourcing is neither a bugaboo nor a panacea. Outsourcing makes sense when an external organization can do a job faster, at higher quality levels, or at cheaper average costs than can be achieved in-house. Comparing in-house costs to the costs of outsourcing is a way of evaluating departmental outputs. Outsourcing some jobs does not mean destroying the department, although staff members tend to think it does.

For more than a century, libraries have practiced some kinds of outsourcing, such as buying Library of Congress printed catalog cards or sending issues of periodicals to a binder to be bound. Many librarians have forgotten that technical services staff members once did those tasks in-house. Similarly, it is acceptable to buy materials on approval plans or hire a specialist to treat materials needing conservation. The question should be, Why is outsourcing *not* considered when local staff are faced with tasks they cannot complete at appropriate quality levels, in a timely manner, and at reasonable costs? Department managers currently have an array of strategies they can employ to do tasks that were once done manually, from scratch, and their libraries might benefit from using more than one strategy to get the work done. Possibilities that involve sending work out or buying something that used to be done in-house from an outside source should not be excluded from consideration.

Decisions to outsource tasks should be made by a knowledgeable department manager (or a group that includes a knowledgeable department manager), meaning someone who can compare outsourcing with other strategies for getting the work done and evaluate the costs of each alternative, in concert with those interested in the outcome. This group of interested parties includes, but is not limited to, library administrators, department staff, and budget overseers. Most notably, the outsourcers themselves should not be involved in making the decisions, although they should be solicited for costs, specifications, and other relevant information.

Once a library begins buying outside services, it has an ethical obligation to give equal consideration to all organizations interested in its business and to treat them fairly in the decision-making process. This means giving each outsourcer the same information about library needs and the same opportunity to present their offerings, and using the same criteria in making a choice.

Jobs that lend themselves to outsourcing:

- Getting rid of a static backlog
- Conducting a preservation survey
- Training staff in new techniques, standards, rules and tools, computer systems, and so on
- Processing an opening-day collection or a large number of new materials in an unfamiliar format
- Cataloging historical collections
- Cataloging specialized materials for which the requisite expertise is not available among departmental staff members, especially foreign-language materials or materials in new physical forms

Evaluating Departmental Outputs

Evaluating departmental outputs is an ongoing responsibility and involves more than counting the numbers of items ordered, cataloged, sent to binders, and so forth. At the least, the department manager should keep track of all of the following and prepare written reports on them at designated times of the year (or, at least, once a year):

- How much work was supposed to be done?
- How much was actually accomplished?

- How long, on average, did each type of work take?
- If there were any bottlenecks in operations, where did they occur and why? How could they be remedied?
- How much did each type of output cost? Did the average cost meet, exceed, or come in at less than expected costs?
- Did the quality of outputs meet expected standards? If not, why not? What can be done to remedy the situation?
- Did the department meet specified goals and objectives for the period (year, quarter, month, week)?

The final question is the key question to be answered, preferably accompanied by documentation to back up whatever claims of success or lack of success are made, along with explanations about why whatever was reported happened. Two things are important about the evaluation report: first, honest conclusions must be drawn, and failures to meet goals should not be swept under the rug; second, recommendations for the future based on the conclusions should be given at the end so readers of the report can see how the manager plans to solve problems or capitalize on successes.

Beyond Departmental Borders

Reporting department activity to library administration is the primary liaison activity the manager must perform. Often, the effectiveness, timeliness, and professionalism of these reports affect the department's future budget and staffing.

The manager serves as the primary liaison with external persons, bodies, and organizations. This may involve correspondence (by mail or e-mail), acting as the library's representative to committees or other bodies, serving on boards, attending meetings, negotiating on behalf of the library, or taking on many kinds of voluntary activities on behalf of the department or the library. When many obligations have to be met, managers often delegate some to an assistant, to unit heads, or to specialist librarians within the department whose expertise is helpful in meeting the commitment. For example, a cataloger might be asked to represent the department to a consortium cataloging committee, or an interlibrary loan librarian might be asked to be the library's representative to a statewide resource-sharing board.

The technical services manager represents the department to some or all of the following:

- Other library departments
- Library higher administration
- Parent body administration
- Peers in other libraries
- Professional associations
- Library vendors and other suppliers (for example, binders, computer systems vendors, material suppliers, and subscription agents)
- Bibliographic networks and other cooperative organizations

Summary

A technical services department manager is responsible for numerous duties involving many different skills. Communication skills are critical because the manager must convey information down the line from higher administration to department staff and up the line from technical services staff to higher administration as well as to the members of the department itself. The manager is responsible for ensuring that staff members understand the policies, goals and objectives, and priorities of the library, and for the staff's successes and failures in implementing them. The department leader is also the person who represents the department to other departments within the library and to groups outside the library. Managers often delegate some responsibilities for staff supervision, data collection, and department representation to assistants, unit heads, or specialist librarians; however, he or she is the one ultimately responsible for the department's successes and failures in meeting its goals and objectives.

Recommended Reading

Christopher, Connie. *Empowering Your Library: A Guide to Improving Service, Productivity, and Participation.* Chicago: American Library Association, 2003.

Laughlin, Sara, et al. *The Library's Continuous Improvement Fieldbook: 29 Ready-to-Use Tools.* Chicago: American Library Association, 2003.

Nelson, Sandra, and June Garcia. *Creating Policies for Results: From Chaos to Clarity.* Chicago: American Library Association, 2003.

Note

1. Abraham A. Schechter's *Basic Book Repair Methods* (Westport, CT: Libraries Unlimited, 1999) originated as a set of procedures to train staff to perform simple book repairs correctly.

CHAPTER 3

Planning Technical Services Policies and Programs

by Peggy Johnson

What Is Planning?

Planning is the process, based on available resources, through which an organization sets goals and develops a strategy to achieve them. Formal planning, along with evaluation techniques to measure progress toward the goals laid out in planning, are now common in most libraries. Informal planning occurs every day because desired outcomes are identified, decisions are made to reach those outcomes, and actions are taken based on those decisions. Formal planning is more systematic and deliberate and generally takes a longer view. It is thoughtful and requires more than building on past successes or intuition. Peter Drucker explains planning as the continuous process of making "decisions systematically and with greatest knowledge of their futurity; organizing systematically

35

the efforts needed to carry out these decisions; and measuring the results of these decisions against the expectations through organized systematic feedback."[1] In addition to identifying what will be done, when it will be done, how it will be done, and who will do it, successful planning should make clear why what will be done is important.

In today's libraries, most planning can be described as strategic because it assumes an environment of constant change and prepares the library to identify and respond to changes in priorities, resources, and other environmental conditions. Strategic planning, although it may look at one-, three-, or five-year increments, does not produce a final, static plan. It remains an open-ended, continuous process that seeks to keep the organization in step with its environment.

Planning for the future requires understanding what the library is doing now, what it would like to be doing in the future given certain probable conditions, and choosing the most reasonable path to that future. For each proposed solution, planning identifies practical alternative solutions and potential barriers. These barriers may be financial, technical, organizational, or political. The planner develops one or more proposals for achieving the most promising alternative—one that is strategic in advancing the library's priorities.

Planning serves several purposes beyond preparing a map to follow. In addition to laying out goals and the strategies for obtaining them, planning fosters organizational learning. It is also a communication tool. Information is shared within the library as part of the planning process and as part of involving staff members in the planning activity. Planning sets a course for the future and provides a means to inform people about that future. By encouraging involvement and the sharing of information, planning activities provide an opportunity for staff members to buy into and support the library's goals. In addition, planning fosters accountability by identifying desired outcomes and providing benchmarks along the path to reach those goals. A plan serves as a management control system. A detailed plan with goals, objectives, and strategies is only one result of formal planning. The process of systematic planning generates its own benefits by creating a vision for the library and engaging people to share that vision.

The concepts of planning on a large scale may seem abstract. Consider the steps in planning a holiday meal to see how these concepts apply to a common experience. Assume the priority is providing a pleasant gathering for relatives. Two goals might be to serve appealing, tasty food and to provide an attractive table. Several objectives, each with action strategies, help reach these goals. For example, in order to serve appealing, tasty food, the host will set objectives: develop a menu, purchase ingredients, and prepare food. Each of these objectives, in turn, will have action strategies. Action strategies necessary to develop a menu might be to survey guests for food allergies, read supermarket advertisements to learn what ingredients are especially fresh or on sale, consult cookbooks for recipes that avoid allergy-causing elements and take advantage of seasonal specials, list all dishes to be prepared and ingredients on hand or that need to be purchased, and develop a shopping list. Each of these strategies will have a date by which it should be accomplished. The objectives of purchasing ingredients and preparing foods will have their own action strategies—all contributing toward the goal of serving appealing, tasty food and leading to a pleasant gathering for relatives. The host will know he has succeeded in reaching the goals for the evening when guests ask for a recipe or wonder aloud when they will be invited for another gathering.

Goals, Objectives, and Action Strategies

Once a clear and shared understanding of library priorities is in place, strategic planning usually consists of creating goals, objectives, and action strategies. Darlene Weingand has defined goals as aspirations or statements of purpose.[2] Goals are not measurable yet provide a focus and adapt to changing conditions. They are broader and more general than objectives.

Objectives are practical, specific, and measurable. They usually include a date by which the objective is to be completed or a specific measure of time within which a task is to be completed. Meaningful objectives are often described as SMART; that is, they are specific, measurable, acceptable, realistic, and time-bound.[3] Action strategies are the detailed activities that lead to attaining objectives.

A critical element in effective planning is measuring success—measuring progress toward achieving the goals identified in the plan and whether or not the goals have been reached. Chapter 9 addresses this topic in detail. Planning not only makes clear goals but also lays out the steps necessary to reach them and the mechanisms for ensuring that the library is on track. It traces progress toward desired interim and final outcomes so that course adjustments can be made when needed to keep the library moving toward desired outcomes within specified time frames.

The Context for Planning in Technical Services

Technical services units and their operations exist within their libraries and in a larger collaborative environment. Planning for technical services occurs in the context of the parent library's mission. Developing a plan in the technical services department that lays out goals, establishes priorities, and aligns resources with reaching those goals is effective only if the goals and priorities match those of the parent library and are consistent with available resources. For example, a cataloging department in an academic library might set a goal to eliminate a cataloging backlog in Scandinavian materials and develop a plan to do so by hiring a temporary cataloger fluent in Scandinavian languages who will be expected to eliminate the backlog in one year. If, however, the library learns that the university has decided to assign a lower priority to Scandinavian studies and to place strong emphasis on growing and strengthening programs in Middle Eastern studies, the library may set a goal to build and provide enhanced access to materials in Hebrew and Arabic. Focusing on providing access to Scandinavian materials instead of Middle Eastern materials places the cataloging plan outside the library's priorities. Plans for technical services units developed in consultation with other units within the library help avoid such problems.

Much of the work in technical services also occurs within the context of widely shared cataloging rules, policies, and standards—and is constrained and facilitated by local automated systems and by practices mandated by shared regional and national systems. The latter includes bibliographic utilities (e.g., OCLC) and the international Program for Cooperative Cataloging (PCC) and its components, Name Authority Cooperative Program (NACO), Monographic Bibliographic Record Cooperative Program (BIBCO), Subject Authority Cooperative Program (SACO), and Cooperative Online Serials Program (CONSER). Another area that defines the work of and planning in technical services are the services and functionalities that publishers, vendors, distributors, binders, and subscription agents provide. Plans to streamline processes, which may involve simplifying or reducing steps, cannot occur without regard to partners in the larger environment in which technical services units operate.

Effective planning requires data. Thus an important element in planning is collecting and analyzing pertinent data. Information is necessary to make informed decisions and plan successfully. Data can highlight trends. For example, declines over time in numbers of journal issues received (perhaps because of title cancellations or a shift to electronic journals) can suggest an opportunity to reallocate staff to other activities. Data can serve as a benchmark and highlight an area in which improvement may be sought. If data show that 20 percent of new monographic receipts arrive shelf-ready, is that amount acceptable? Should a plan be developed to increase the percentage?

Data are also necessary to measure progress toward attaining goals. Perhaps a library has set a goal to eliminate a cataloging backlog and move all new monographs through the cataloging unit within three months of receipt. The plan might involve different approaches to cataloging in order to reach this goal. They might include increasing the volume of original cataloging or of base- or core-level records, outsourcing cataloging of some items, purchasing records from a vendor, or a combination of approaches. If, when the plan is developed, materials sit on a cataloging hold shelf for as long as eighteen months, data can be gathered that track a steady decline in holding period until the goal of no more than three months is reached.

Librarians have become masters at counting things (titles cataloged, dollars expended, serial issues checked in, volumes bound, records loaded, orders placed), with a focus on counting inputs and outputs. They have had some success in measuring throughput (for example, number of days between receipt of a book and its availability through the catalog or on the shelf). Both inputs and outputs often can be generated automatically, though many library staff members continue to count and measure manually.

Librarians, including their technical services units, have had less success measuring qualitative factors. What is a good catalog record? How important are analytics? How many subject headings or added entries are enough? Will outsourcing tasks (for example, authority control as a postcataloging process) provide the quality of work required by a library? Equally challenging is determining how long a particular task takes and, following on that calculation, how much a task costs. Measuring costs requires consistency in defining terms and procedures and in collecting production and cost details. Differences in quality standards are an important factor in variations in production or quantity and, therefore, in production costs. Nevertheless, librarians should seek data in these areas in order to have enough information to consider alternatives and make informed decisions in the planning process.

Developing Goals, Objectives, and Action Strategies

Planning begins with understanding of priorities and current processes. For illustration, begin with a commonly held library priority—providing timely access to materials selected for addition to the library's collection. The technical services unit has a central role in supporting this library-wide priority. To succeed, technical services managers will develop effective goals, objectives, and action strategies. Developing these components of a plan requires knowing how tasks are currently handled and how work is assigned. Frequently used resources to build such knowledge are work-flow diagrams, organizational charts, job descriptions, counts of inputs and outputs, procedural manuals, and budgets.

While much of the focus in developing a plan to increase timely access will most likely be on improving organizational performance, attention will also be given to areas in which planning crosses divisions and departments in the library and where decisions involve services provided by external agents. The following examples of goals, objectives, and action strategies are not complete but are intended to be representative of the elements in a plan. More details are provided with the first goal.

One goal could be to improve processes so that all monographic orders submitted to an acquisition unit are placed within twenty-four hours of receipt. An objective to support this goal might be to expand direct online order placement so that 50 percent of all book orders are placed online with a single vendor by the end of the calendar year. Action strategies in support of this objective might include the following:

> During month 1, implement the policy that all English-language orders will be placed with a single vendor.
>
> During months 1 and 2, develop technical specifications with the vendor to accommodate direct online order placement.
>
> Simultaneously, consult with local automated systems staff to devise a method for batch loading order records supplied by the vendor.
>
> During month 3, work with collection development librarians to develop a process for and encourage (or mandate) consistent e-mail transmission of selections to acquisitions staff.
>
> During month 4, test new processes.
>
> During month 5, implement the new processes.
>
> During month 6 and at regular intervals, collect data and evaluate success in reaching the objective of placing 50 percent of all book orders directly online with a single vendor.

Flowcharts are diagrams that map a sequence of steps in a process. They originated in computer science to aid programming by documenting sequentially each action a computer takes, the points at which either/or responses occur, the resulting alternative paths, and the interrelationships of steps. Process flowcharts have become a valuable tool in process improvement. An effective flowchart will document all the steps in a process with the goal of identifying and eliminating unnecessary steps, redundancies, and bottlenecks and pinpointing where new or different steps can lead to improvement. Flowcharts use a set of standard symbols to represent the types of operations being performed, thus ensuring a common approach to interpretation. Many word processing software packages include these standard symbols. Free and commercial flowcharting software packages are also available. *Business Process Improvement Toolbox,* by Bjørn Andersen (Milwaukee: ASQ Quality Press, 1999), is a useful resource for process flowcharting. Opposite is an example of a simple flowchart.

Another objective might be to streamline order placement processes and improve work flow within technical services. The following action strategies might support that objective:

Create a specific e-mail box or paper in-box or both to receive all the selectors' order requests.

Assign twice-daily responsibility for checking the boxes and placing orders to one individual and a backup.

Another goal might address shortening the time between the date a book is published and its availability for circulation. One objective toward this goal might be to expand use of a vendor approval plan so that the vendor selects more books for the library based on a pro-

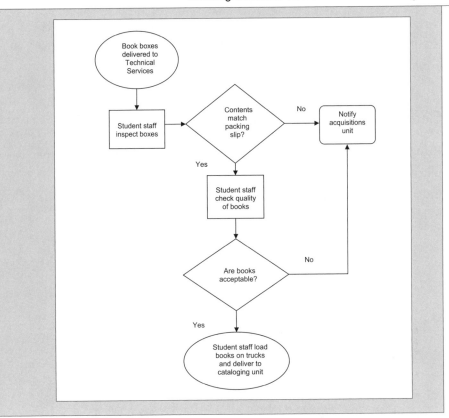

file or criteria developed by library representatives. Action strategies in this area would require heavy involvement of appropriate library staff to revise and expand the approval-plan profile and would depend on available funding. Another objective to advance the goal of shortening the time between publication and availability would be to increase the number of books, both those from the approval plan and those selected title by title, that are shipped to the library shelf-ready (i.e., with spine labels, antitheft target strips, and all other required preparation), with full catalog records suitable for batch loading into the local automated system. Another objective might be to work with the circulation unit to ensure that books sent from the cataloging unit are shelved promptly. Moving in these directions could dramatically reduce the length of time between the date a book is published, the date it is received by the library, and when it is both intellectually accessible (through the catalog) and physically accessible (shelved in the collection).

Elements in a Successful Plan

Plans vary in the level of detail they contain, depending on the complexity of the project or initiative, its duration, and the number of individuals and units involved. At a minimum, a plan will present the following:

- Intended result or results (economies, efficiencies, improvements)
- Steps to be taken, including sequence and dependencies
- Time frame
- Resources required (funding, staff, technology, etc.)
- Budget (sources of funds and projected expenses by category)
- Who is responsible for actions
- Who is accountable for success
- Who will report progress and completion and to whom
- Implications for and effects on other units, organizations, or individuals
- Benchmarks against which to measure progress

Documenting a plan in writing is critical. The level of detail will depend on the project or initiative. Some managers find Gantt charts useful. A Gantt chart is a scheduling tool that displays the status of a project's tasks by representing each task's duration as a horizontal line. The ends of a line correspond to a task's start and end dates. Commercial software, such as Microsoft Project, may be used. Such software is helpful in identifying dependencies and automatically recalculating dates if one aspect of the project takes longer than expected. For less complex plans, a spreadsheet program, such as Excel, can serve equally well. A simple narrative is another option, though to be useful it will probably need to include a fairly detailed budget. Regular reports to managers and stakeholders demonstrating progress and accomplishments are part of a project's documentation.

An effective plan is flexible. It can be changed to match changes in circumstances, available resources, departmental and library priorities, the extent to which accomplishments match the prescribed time frame, and so on. Often plans have built-in contingencies. For example, a library may operate in an institutional environment in which all acquisitions funds must be expended by the end of the fiscal year and all unexpended funds automatically revert to a central budget. In such circumstances, appropriate managers will work with selectors to develop a plan to ensure that all orders are received by a specified time before the end of the fiscal year. Staff members will be assigned responsibility to ensure that all invoices are approved for payment in time for accounting staff to expend all funds previously encumbered in the placement of orders. A contingency plan will also be developed to identify other trained staff who will step in and make sure all invoices are approved before the cutoff date in the event that an acquisitions staff person becomes ill.

Planning as Consultation

Planning is a not a solitary activity. While one individual, usually a manager, unit head, or senior administrator, has final authority and ultimate accountability, planning is collaborative. Planning involves wide consultation both within the unit or department and across organizational boundaries. The strategy must be acceptable to stakeholders as well as decision makers. Often staff members doing the work know more about the tasks, pressures, and options than managers do. Wide consultation ensures that no ugly surprises will occur as the plan and its activities are implemented. Good communication is essential in developing a plan and in adjusting it as it moves forward. Participation both empowers and motivates those who are involved in developing the plan. They are the ones on whom its success depends. John Bryson writes that the strategy selected "must be technically workable, politically everal years after implementing an integrated library system and retrospective conversion of all cataloging records, a technical services department head noted that valuable floor space in the cataloging unit was being occupied by cabinets of shelflist files: one block of Dewey shelflist card cabinets and a larger block of Library of Congress (LC) shelflist card cabinets. The department head asked the catalogers, acquisitions staff, and circulation staff if they used the card shelflist files. All said they might need to look up something once every three or four months, at most. While not yet ready to dispose of the files, they agreed the cabinets could be moved to a storage area in the basement. The technical services department head made arrangements for facilities staff to move the files and began working with a task group to plan how the soon-to-be-opened space might be put to best use. On the day the movers arrived, the head of cataloging stood in front of the LC shelflist card cabinets and loudly refused to let anyone touch them. She was willing to let the Dewey files be moved, but she could not imagine the LC shelflist cards being put outside her immediate reach. While the department head had consulted widely and thought she had complete agreement, she had failed to confirm the exact details of what she thought had been a joint decision. Due to the lack of clarity, the differing assumptions of the head of technical services and the head of cataloging resulted in an unpleasant situation that caused frustration and derailed planning.

acceptable to key stakeholders, and must accord with the organization's philosophy and core values."[4]

Planning involves developing and motivating individuals. Some people tend to invest more time in fulfilling objectives and accomplishing tasks related to their own particular areas and interests, thus losing sight of the priorities established for the unit. For example, the top objective of a catalog department may be to catalog all current, incoming materials as quickly as possible. However, some staff members may give higher priority to other objectives (such as getting rid of a backlog or reclassifying portions of the already-classified collection) and thus cause the department to fall behind in achieving its primary objective.

Many people think only in terms of carrying out tasks, not in terms of achieving objectives. Some individuals focus more on the means and methods of a task or on executing their specific responsibilities and may be unable to describe the goals and objectives of their unit or library. Libraries with clear and widely understood goals and objectives tend to have higher staff morale. Ensuring that staff understand the library's goals and objectives, actively participating in their development, and feeling responsible for their accomplishment helps foster support of and loyalty to the plan. Establishing written goals and objectives and communicating them to technical services staff members and the rest of the organization encourages individuals to think through logical courses of action and provides a yardstick for measuring their own decision making and activities.

Planning as a Continuous Activity

Much of the planning in technical services is not project driven and may be perceived as less formal or structured because it is an ongoing process that involves constant course adjustments. For example, an individual in a serials unit may resign. The manager, in deciding what to do, will consider the following points:

- Has the work this person was originally hired to do changed?
- Does another area have a greater volume of work that requires additional staffing?
- Should the same position be reposted or should a different position be created?
- Is a different skill set necessary in the new position?
- Can the salary line be deployed in another way, perhaps for hiring a temporary employee for a special project or purchasing contract cataloging or other services or records?

The central question confronting the manager is one all managers constantly face—how to allocate resources in response to changes in the environment while keeping in mind the library's mission and priorities. While not project based, continuous planning is always programmatic because it keeps in mind the priorities of the organization and seeks to advance the goals and objectives that support those priorities.

Good managers, although they may not be aware of doing so, develop a coherent and defensible basis for their decision making. They make decisions in light of the future consequences. Peter Drucker writes of planning as improving the "futurity" of decisions.[5] Effective managers are constantly considering how they can improve performance within their unit and how they can explain their choices to reach this end. Planning is a continuous cycle, as illustrated in figure 3.1. A manager develops a plan, implements it, measures success against benchmarks or targets (which may be qualitative or quantitative), adjusts the plan when necessary to stay on course to reach the plan's goal or goals, and resumes planning objectives and action strategies for the next phase or project. Much of planning and decision making comes down to continuously balancing two objectives: decreasing or holding costs steady and improving effectiveness of services. The tension between these two aims is constant. New priorities and new projects will place stresses on

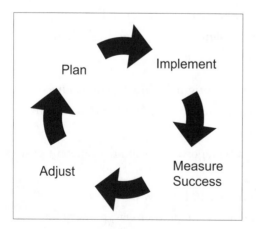

Figure 3.1   Planning cycle

these two objectives, requiring frequent adjustments to bring them into balance.

Procedures, Policies, Rules, and Standards

A chapter on planning would be incomplete if it did not address the role of procedures, policies, rules, and standards in technical services. Procedures tend to be local and specific to a single library. They are sequential lists of what is to be done and provide a particular course of action intended to achieve a result. They set a means of performing tasks to ensure uniformity and consistency. "Procedure for Importing and Overlaying Records" (see fig. 3.2) and "Procedure for Creating a Vendor Record in the Acquisitions Model" are common examples. Procedures are specific lists of the processes to be followed. Procedures are subordinate to policies.

Policies are an "overall guide setting up boundaries that supply the general limits and direction in which managerial action will take place."[6] Policies remain in effect until they are revised or rescinded. A typical policy might require that all English-language monographs be ordered from a single, specified vendor and lay out when exceptions are permitted. Policies rule out the need to consider the same questions again and again; they ensure a degree of consistency and contribute toward efficiency. Policies serve as guides and allow some discretion and latitude. Policies, often cumulated into manuals, usually lay out an organization's decisions in relation to its goals and objectives. A policy manual serves as a record, a decision-making guide, and a way of communicating within the organization. It also serves as a historical record of decisions made.

Procedures and policies should be flexible. They should be subject to change as new needs arise and should be reviewed and revised regularly. Procedures and policies are often revised as part of planning activities. More efficient ways are identified, so the procedures for importing and overlaying records, for example, are revised. When an automated system is upgraded with a new version, the procedure for

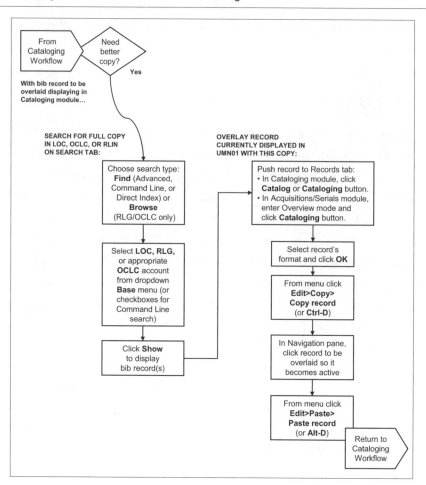

Figure 3.2   Bibliographic overlay work flow

creating a vendor record will change, thus necessitating new procedures. A vendor offers to increase its discount on monographs if the
number of orders increases, so the library creates a policy to consolidate
as many orders as possible with that vendor.

Rules spell out a required course of action or conduct that must be
followed. A rule prescribes a specific action for a given situation and creates uniformity of action. Rules ensure stable, consistent, and uniform
behavior by individuals in accomplishing tasks. Rules are also guides,
but they allow little or no discretion or initiative in their application.

The *Anglo-American Cataloguing Rules* (AACR) are the most familiar rules followed by technical services librarians. They ensure consistency in the local catalog and in national, shared catalogs. Rules are subject to interpretation. Rule interpretations made by the Library of Congress and published for the rest of the library community serve as guides to national practice in interpreting AACR. Individual libraries may supplement them with locally applied interpretations.

L ibraries are in a unique position to take advantage of standards as compared to many other institutions. Unlike banks, manufacturers, or retail businesses, libraries are not in competition with each other. And unlike elementary schools, city governments, or non-profits in general, libraries have a strong professional connection that promulgates standards."

Source: Karen Coyle, "Managing Technology: Libraries and Standards," *Journal of Academic Librarianship* 31, no. 4 (July 2005): 373–76.

Standards are technical specifications or criteria describing the characteristics of a product, such as size, quality, performance, or safety. They describe the criteria or standards of performance that must be attained. The Machine-Readable Cataloging (MARC) formats for bibliographic records, authority records, and holdings records are standards for the representation and communication of bibliographic and related information in machine-readable form. The MARC standards provide for consistent formatting of cataloging records and are essential for automated manipulation of these records. Standards are not subject to local interpretation. Adherence to prescribed national and international standards is necessary for much of the work that technical services librarians do. Electronic Data Interchange (EDI) standards define the specifications for computer-to-computer transmission of data and are necessary for such activities as automated transmission of serials claims to vendors and suppliers.

Planning projects and planning the annual work flow of a technical services unit both depend on procedures, policies, rules, and standards. Part of the consultation process that contributes to the development and revision of plans entails taking note of procedures, policies, rules, and standards, revising those that can be revised, and adjusting the plan to accommodate those that cannot.

Summary

Planning in technical services addresses three fundamental questions: What are the library's mission and priorities? What are the goals, objectives, and strategies in technical services that will advance that mission and achieve those priorities? How do the unit and its staff members measure results and know if they are on track? Plans are flexible because they adjust and adapt in response to changes in the environment in which the technical services unit operates. Planning is most effective if it occurs in a consultative environment, not only crossing organizational boundaries but actively engaging staff members in the unit. Planning should be done with staff input, not arbitrarily imposed on staff, or it runs the risk of not being understood or supported. Planning is continuous and cyclical, requiring adjustments as conditions change. Procedures, policies, rules, and standards cannot be ignored in planning. Procedures and policies may require revision, and new ones may be required. Rules and standards, by their nature prescriptive, may require changes in plans to accommodate compliance. Planning is the process that sets the future course for technical services. In an age of constant change, effective planning is essential.

Recommended Reading

Curzon, Susan Carol. *Managing Change: A How-to-Do-It Manual for Libraries.* New York: Neal-Schuman, 2005.

Eden, Bradford Lee, ed. *Innovative Redesign and Reorganization of Library Technical Services: Paths for the Future and Case Studies.* Westport, CT: Libraries Unlimited, 2004.

Greever, Karen E., and Debra K. Andreadis. "Technical Services Work Redesign across Two College Libraries." *Technical Services Quarterly* 24, no. 2 (2006): 45–54.

Hayes, Robert M. *Models for Library Management, Decision-Making, and Planning.* San Diego: Academic Press, 2001.

Kaplan, Robert S., and David P. Norton. "Using the Balanced Scorecard as a Strategic Management System." *Harvard Business Review* 74, no. 1 (January/February 1996): 75–85.

Matthews, Joseph R. *Strategic Planning and Management for Library Managers.* Westport, CT: Libraries Unlimited, 2005.

Winston, Mark D., and Tara Hoffman. "Project Management in Libraries." *Journal of Library Administration* 42, no. 1 (2005): 51–61.

Zhang, Ying, and Connie Bishop. "Project Management Tools for Libraries: A Planning and Implementation Model Using Microsoft Project 2000." *Information Technology and Libraries* 24, no. 3 (September 2005): 147–52.

Notes

1. Peter F. Drucker, *Management: Tasks, Responsibilities, Practices* (New York: Harper and Row, 1973), 175.

2. Darlene E. Weingand, *Marketing/Planning Library and Information Services,* 2nd ed. (Englewood, CO: Libraries Unlimited, 1999).

3. Vivek Nanda, *Quality Management System Handbook for Product Development Companies* (Boca Raton, FL: CRC Press, 2005).

4. John M. Bryson, *Strategic Planning for Public and Nonprofit Organizations* (San Francisco: Jossey-Bass, 1989), 179.

5. Drucker, *Management,* 125.

6. M. Valliant Higginson, "Putting Policies in Context," in *Business Policy,* ed. Alfred Gross and Walter Dross, 230 (New York: Ronald Press, 1967).

CHAPTER 4

Vendor Relations

✧ Buying for Technical Services
✧ Interactions with Vendors
✧ Evaluating Vendor Performance
✧ Summary

LIBRARIES rely on outside vendors—that is, commercial or nonprofit organizations unaffiliated with the libraries themselves or their parent bodies—for numerous products and services. Purchases may include anything from materials for the collections to computer networking, library catalogs, or Internet services, to name just a few of the possible examples. Even when a library's bibliographic products and services are produced in-house by technical services staff members, they may be supported by, created through, or displayed in systems, products, or services that the library purchases from outside vendors.

Managing these purchases and integrating them with internal library work flows are important tasks for the technical services manager. This chapter describes a number of products and services that libraries typically purchase from outside vendors, gives an overview of the interactions these purchases involve, and suggests ways of evaluating vendor performance.

Buying for Technical Services

Each part of technical services (acquisition of materials, cataloging and classification, processing, binding and preservation, etc.) has elements that libraries have traditionally obtained from outside sources. Examples in acquisitions include buying materials from wholesalers (or jobbers) and subscription agents, who enable their library customers to buy from a single source titles issued by many publishers. Some also supply processing and cataloging for the materials they sell. Examples in cataloging include buying computerized catalog records (formerly physical cards) from sources as varied as the Library of Congress, H. W. Wilson, and OCLC, the nonprofit shared bibliographic network, among others. Examples in preservation include outsourcing of binding and rebinding to professional binderies. A relatively recent development is the buying of access to online databases from outside vendors, third parties who behave much like subscription agents, aggregating large numbers of titles into a single product having a uniform computer-user interface. The range of products and services that may be purchased by a technical services unit is too vast to discuss in a limited number of pages, so this chapter offers an introduction to the most common types of purchasing.

Acquisition of Materials

Wholesalers and jobbers generally deal with monographic titles, while subscription agents deal with periodicals and other serially issued titles. Although some wholesalers limit their inventories to books, most also provide popular audiovisual materials, such as sound recordings, educational films, and video recordings. Some vendors of library materials specialize in subject areas (e.g., law, science-technology-medicine, or foreign-language materials); others cater to particular clienteles, such as schools or small public libraries.

Library acquisitions units generally do not purchase each desired title from its publisher or producer; they group titles into orders based on chronology, subject, department, audience, or whatever criterion they choose and send the orders to the appropriate vendors to be fulfilled. The in-house acquisitions unit is the library's liaison with the vendor, writing and sending the orders, maintaining order files, receiving the materials and checking to be sure they are correct, and paying for them. For libraries that buy thousands or tens of thousands of monographic titles annually, working with wholesalers is a major effort requiring a large staff.

THE ISBN

Standard numbers for books and booklike materials (monographic publications or single issues of annuals or other continuations) are known as International Standard Book Numbers, abbreviated ISBN. In the United States, ISBN is administered by the R. R. Bowker Publishing Company at an office in New Providence, New Jersey. Any publisher can apply for an ISBN identifier and purchase bar codes to assign to its publications. Sometimes ISBNs are assigned to materials other than books.

Until recently, the ISBN consisted of ten characters, either all digits or nine digits and an X, divided into the following four groups separated by hyphens:

1. A single digit representing the geographic origin of the material (0 and 1 represent English-speaking countries)
2. A group of numbers identifying the publisher
3. A sequential number assigned by the publisher to each publication it issues
4. A check digit that can be either a number between 0 and 9 or an X representing the number 10

Groups 2 and 3 consist of different combinations of eight digits (2 digits and 6 digits, 3 and 5, 4 and 4, 5 and 3, or 6 and 2), depending on whether a publisher issues many titles or only a few. For a publisher that is prolific, group 2 may contain as few as two digits and group 3 may contain as many as six digits, which will allow up to 999,999 sequential numbers to be assigned to publications. If the publisher is likely to produce very few titles, group 2 may contain up to six digits and group 3 may contain as few as two digits. Thus, for a small publisher, if group 2 contains five digits and group 3 contains three, up to 999 publications could be identified.

Today, ISBNs consist of thirteen digits. An internationally recognized three-digit prefix—978 or 979—is added before the country code. Ten-digit ISBNs can be converted to thirteen digits by adding 978 and changing the check digit. ISBNs that begin with 979 cannot be converted back to ten digits.

THE ISSN

Standard numbers for serial publications are known as International Standard Serial Numbers, abbreviated ISSN. An ISSN consists of eight characters in the form nnnn-nnnc, where n is a digit between 0 and 9, and c is a check digit that can be either a digit between 0 and 9 or an X representing the number 10. International Standard Serial Numbers are consecutive numbers assigned at random by one of more than seventy ISSN agencies located throughout the world. The ISSN international headquarters is in Paris; the office for the United States is at the Library of Congress.

Buying through wholesale vendors saves libraries the much bigger job of repeating the entire acquisition process from beginning to end with individual publishers each time a title is purchased. Very large libraries have gone a step beyond merely buying from wholesale vendors by devising methods of automatic buying with their vendors. Two such strategies are blanket orders and approval plans. In the former, libraries obtain all new titles issued by designated publishing houses; in the latter, libraries obtain all new titles that meet specific criteria, such as those bearing particular Dewey Decimal or Library of Congress call numbers.[1] Automatic buying is intended to ensure that libraries obtain all the materials they want as quickly as possible and that desired titles are not missed because librarians fail to order them.

Similarly, when libraries buy serial titles, the desired subscriptions are grouped and submitted to a subscription agent, who handles the details of placing or renewing subscriptions, claiming missing issues, and so forth on behalf of libraries' serials units. Members of the serials units work with their agents to ensure that desired titles are ordered and renewed, titles no longer wanted are dropped, issues arrive on time, and so on. Again, the value of using a subscription agent is in the economies gained by dealing with one source and paying one bill for all titles ordered, thus avoiding the need to go through the entire buying and receiving cycle for each new title and dealing with each publisher separately.

Although products are involved, namely, the materials being purchased, libraries actually are buying wholesaling services from companies that serve as brokers between the publishers that issue materials and the libraries who buy them. Because of the nature of brokering products and performing services, dealings with wholesalers, subscription agents, and database providers are (or should be) governed by contracts that spell out the terms of the deal: what the wholesaler/agent/provider will supply and under what specific terms and conditions (costs, payment terms, order turnaround time, error correction, return policies, etc.), and what the library will get and under what specific terms and conditions (ordering and invoicing requirements, customer services, user support, training, etc.). Contract issues are discussed in more detail later in this chapter.

Catalogs and Cataloging

Two kinds of products have long been purchased by library cataloging departments: tools such as subject heading lists, classifications, and descriptive cataloging rules and catalog records that they incorporate into their local catalogs. These kinds of products are still being purchased, although they have changed considerably since the advent of computers. In addition, today cataloging departments also purchase the catalogs themselves, that is, computer-based catalog display systems called Online Public Access Catalogs (OPACs), into which they enter the catalog records they buy and those they create originally, from scratch.

Card catalogs were the norm in libraries from the end of the nineteenth century to the last quarter of the twentieth century. At first, the cards were written by hand. Early in the twentieth century, the Library of Congress (LC) began selling printed cards for the books it cataloged, which immediately became popular with academic libraries of all sizes as well as medium-sized and large public libraries. In the 1930s, the H. W. Wilson Company (Wilson) began selling less detailed catalog records on cards for titles intended for small public and school libraries.

Computerized cataloging was developed at LC in the 1960s and early 1970s. The LC encoding system, known as MARC, was adopted by the OCLC bibliographic network, the first shared cataloging network, and later by other networks. It soon became a nationwide standard. The Library of Congress switched from storing catalog records on printed cards to computerized storage and distribution systems and continued to sell both cards and computerized catalog products to libraries. Simultaneously with developments at LC, the OCLC network, which began in Ohio, quickly branched out beyond state and national borders. It has become the world's largest bibliographic network, combining first with the Western Library Network and later with the Research Libraries Information Network.

On behalf of its members, OCLC buys and adds LC MARC records to its WorldCat database as well as the original catalog records produced in the catalog departments of all its members. It also adds MARC records obtained from national libraries around the world. Members of OCLC share access to this enormous database, paying for services that go far beyond cataloging to interlibrary loan and reference information services.

In the 1990s, OCLC initiated a cataloging service for libraries called PromptCat that has since become a separate commercial entity. Libraries can hire PromptCat to catalog their new materials in place of doing it themselves, in which case they have acquisitions vendors send the materials to PromptCat first and receive them after they are cataloged. Wholesalers of library materials are engaging PromptCat catalogers to supply standard network cataloging for the materials they sell, combining product acquisition and cataloging services into one smooth operation.

For libraries that continue to catalog new materials in-house, LC and Wilson publish lists of authorized subject headings to be assigned to them. Library of Congress also publishes its classification schedules, which many academic libraries use for original classification. Most school and public libraries buy and use the *Dewey Decimal Classification,* published by OCLC/Forest Press. All of these products are available as printed volumes, in online versions, and, in some instances, in off-line electronic forms, such as CD-ROM or magnetic tape, that can be loaded into a local cataloging system automatically.

No discussion of cataloging tools purchased from outside vendors is complete without mentioning the descriptive cataloging rules known at this writing as the *Anglo-American Cataloguing Rules,* 2nd edition (AACR2).[2] Subject heading lists and classification schedules govern parts of the catalog record that relate to the content of materials. Rules explaining how to prepare descriptions of materials, such as exact titles, authors, editions, publication/distribution information, and the like, are found in AACR2. This code undergoes constant (the rule makers call it *dynamic*) revision, which means libraries must buy updates as they are issued or subscribe to online updates. To accommodate this, the printed version of AACR2 is no longer sold in bound volumes but as loose-leaf binder pages. In addition, interpretations of the rules and assistance in applying them correctly are available from LC in the form of *Library of Congress Rule Interpretations*[3] as well as from teaching manuals (see the recommended reading at the end of this chapter).

As buyers of cataloging tools such as subject heading lists, classification schedules, and cataloging rules, libraries are like all buyers of publications. They pay money for a copy or a subscription, and they own the product that is delivered. In the library world, however, users of what have become standard professional tools also have opportunities to lobby for attention and assistance from the publishers. To take advantage of these opportunities, local librarians need to join the professional associations that have committees overseeing the tools on

The cost of cataloging can vary widely from one library to another, and there are no standards for what cataloging should cost. Some library directors and heads of cataloging are ill informed about how much they pay for cataloging. Some years ago, a consultant was hired to investigate a proposal to merge cataloging operations then based at the individual campuses of a large college library system into a centralized unit located at the administrative headquarters. The consultant interviewed each campus library director to learn how he or she viewed the cataloging unit and what centralization could achieve, and to solicit suggestions. Some directors thought their catalogers were overburdened and underpaid. Others said they might achieve small reductions in costs. None suggested radical improvements. None wanted to try outsourcing. Most, though not all, opposed centralizing. Next, the consultant determined the average cost of cataloging for each campus. She obtained data showing how much cataloging each campus produced in the previous year, how many cataloging staff-hours were logged, and what they cost. To account for benefits, a percentage was added to the salary figures for full-time catalogers but not for part-timers, although some received minor benefits. When the data were processed, startling results emerged—an average catalog record cost just over $5 at the campus with the lowest cost and several hundred dollars at the campus with the highest cost, with most costs in the $25 to $50 range. Given that the bulk of cataloging at all campuses was copy cataloging, the results made the centralization plan look very sensible. The consultant started a process of discussing and exploring changes, but for many of the campuses the road ahead looked rough.

behalf of all libraries, such as the Association for Library Collections and Technical Services (ALCTS),[4] and volunteer their services.

When it comes to cataloging and online bibliographic network services, on the other hand, libraries are buying ongoing services, and contracts need to spell out the terms of the deals. The OCLC and other bibliographic networks have complex pricing structures based on basic service packages and optional add-ons. A wise buyer will distinguish between library needs and wants before signing up for all the attractive add-ons and will consult with public service counterparts so a library's overall package of network services meets all of its needs, not just those of a single department.

Libraries that contribute large numbers of unique new catalog records to a shared database or supply more interlibrary loan titles to their partners than they borrow may be rewarded with small bonuses that help defray the cost of belonging to a network. Cataloging and network services are not inexpensive. Part of a department manager's job is to figure out when buying cataloging and network services is less costly than do-it-yourself production within the library or other alternatives, present the facts to the library administration, and stand ready to implement the final decisions.

Binding and Preservation

Most libraries have not maintained in-house binderies for decades, choosing instead to send materials to commercial binderies for initial binding (often done for materials such as paperbound books and journal volumes) and rebinding of worn or damaged books. Preparation of materials for the bindery involves deciding how the binding is to be done (hot or cold gluing or sewing), the type of cover (heavy duty, standard, or custom materials), and even the kind of lettering and the way it will appear on the spine of the bound volume. These details must be conveyed to the binder so work can be done correctly. Some libraries give great latitude to their binders in making such decisions, but if they do they must be ready to live with the results and cannot complain if different choices would have been preferred.

In binding, turnaround time can be significant because libraries lose immediate access to their materials during the whole process. Colleges and universities that schedule classes throughout the year can find themselves unable to serve library patrons adequately if binding takes a long time. Technical services managers, if they are responsible for negotiating binding contracts, need to pay attention to this matter. Contracts can specify maximum turnaround times as well as binding specifications and other details, but when speedy service is required, costs may well rise accordingly.

Interactions with Vendors

Library-vendor interactions include, but are not limited to, initial agreements and contracts to buy or lease products or services; ongoing communication between the partners concerning purchases or leases, charges, and payments; and provision of information about changes in products, services, costs, and contracts likely to affect future dealings.

Negotiating Contracts and Other Initial Agreements

In the less complicated world of the nineteenth century, some vendors prided themselves on not needing a legal contract to make them live up to their promises. That world, if it ever existed, is long gone. Now few librarians would commit to pay a vendor large sums of money without a legal document ensuring the terms of the deal. Moreover, librarians do not buy today's electronic materials and some commercial computer systems outright but arrange, instead, for the library to have access to the materials or systems for the duration of a contract. Vendors anticipate that once libraries subscribe to their products and services, they will resubscribe or expand the contracts in the future. Librarians want members of the public to use the services heavily or like using them well enough themselves to justify their costs and ongoing expenditures. As collections shift from purchased hard-copy editions of materials to leased digitized editions, negotiating skills become more and more important.

Ongoing Communications

Network vendors and vendors of computer systems often have several levels of ongoing communication with customers. Specific types include, but are not limited to, initial installation and training in use of the system; user support, including tangible support for groups of users sharing common interests; system support, including online, telephone hotline, and on-site field services; and programs of research and development that result in the regular introduction of new features, products, and services.

Materials vendors traditionally employed field service representatives to call on customers, bringing the latest news about products and services and responding to customer complaints or trying to help customers solve their problems, whether or not the vendor was directly involved. Field service representatives generated goodwill, often bringing little gifts such as notepads, pens, and other useful trinkets bearing vendors' names. They also collected information that helped their employers understand customer concerns and views. In recent years, however, with the rise of e-mail and online messaging, the isolation of individual libraries and the concomitant need for face-to-face interactions with representatives has diminished. Added to this are the rising costs of maintaining a corps of representatives. In most cases, fewer in-person visits and more online communications have become the norm.

Charges and Payments

An important vendor-librarian interaction involves the exchange of money: vendors bill and libraries pay. How efficiently the billing and payment processes work (or fail to work) can be a source of friction. Astute department managers can do three things to minimize unnecessary friction and help avoid penalties for failure to pay bills within contractual deadlines:

1. Learn exactly how vendors' billing procedures work and explain them to the library's finance administrators

2. Request that their library avoid unnecessary billing procedures that delay or add costs to the submission of payments (for example, requiring that numerous copies be submitted for approval to different offices) but stand ready to explain necessary library procedures to the vendor

3. Facilitate prompt payment of bills by sending all needed information to library financial offices on time

Problems originate on the vendor side as well as in the libraries. Failure to submit bills promptly, billing errors, failure to supply products or services as specified by contracts, and errors in the products or services supplied are all reasons why libraries feel justified in delaying payments until the outstanding problems are resolved. In such instances, communication between the partners is essential to ascertain what has occurred, solve the problems as quickly as possible, agree on appropriate steps to satisfy current obligations, and prevent more problems.

When problems occur, wise managers keep an open mind before deciding what has gone wrong, what needs to be done to resolve it, and who is responsible. They try to determine the facts and do their best to avoid miscommunication or premature finger-pointing. They realize that vendors who have supplied products or performed services properly deserve to be paid without unnecessary delay.

Forecasts and Other Information Services

Among the value-added materials suppliers traditionally provide are forecasts of price changes for the coming year; lists of forthcoming titles; suggested selections for specific types of libraries, audiences, or areas of interest; and offers to provide entire "opening-day" collections of materials not previously held by customers. (An example of this last type of service is a collection of videos for a library that previously had none.)

Information coming from knowledgeable, reliable vendors is a valuable tool for planning and budgeting. Materials budgets may be computed on the basis of vendors' forecasts. Lists of forthcoming titles and suggested selections, while primarily aimed at helping collection development librarians, also benefit acquisitions and cataloging staff members as they make plans to accommodate likely work flows.

Ethical Issues

Technical services managers should be aware of the potential for violating professional ethics by inappropriately accepting gifts or benefiting personally from interactions with vendors. There is a simple test to avoid inadvertent infractions of this sort: managers need only ask if taking a gift will benefit their libraries or themselves and refuse if the beneficiary is themselves. The size of a gift is sometimes used to establish propriety, but that is not the issue. An inexpensive gift pen bearing a vendor's name benefits the library if it stays in the library and is used for work in the office, but if the pen ends up in the book bag of the librarian's child and is used for the child's schoolwork, it benefits the librarian.

Evaluating Vendor Performance

Technical services managers are responsible for keeping track of vendors' performance and ensuring that it meets the terms of the contracts vendors and libraries have signed. Fulfilling the contract is what managers can expect and demand, if necessary. Managers also must keep track of their own obligations (on behalf of their libraries) to the vendors, documenting that these have been met as well.

Problems occur when contract details fail to specify performance criteria used in evaluation. For example, if a contract says nothing about turnaround times, discounts, quality levels, and the like, there is little recourse when the wrong materials are delivered or the right ones are not delivered promptly, when charges are much higher than expected, or when cataloging records contain numerous errors. Faced with problems like these, managers need to gather evidence to document what has happened, present it to the vendors and their library administration, and see if solutions can be found that address the problems and meet library needs.

Vendors should be informed that appropriate criteria and objective measures will be used to evaluate their performance throughout the duration of their contracts. Hearsay and anecdotal evidence cannot prove bad performance, but well-documented errors, tardiness, overcharges, or other contract infractions provide the evidence needed to support claims for redress. Tolerance for human error is part and parcel of dealing with any organization, and good managers give vendors opportunities to rectify poor performance. However, vendors that perpetually make deliveries later than promised, make numerous errors, supply substandard or incorrect products, bill more than contracts allow, or otherwise fail in their obligations must be replaced.

Summary

Technical services managers frequently work with a range of outside vendors from which they buy materials or access to electronic materials; cataloging data, electronic catalogs, and network services; binding and processing services; and other products and services. Purchases from and leases with outside vendors require negotiating proper contracts, overseeing contract implementation, and evaluating vendor performance, all of which fall under the manager's list of responsibilities. Good managers work to ensure that their libraries obtain the products and services they need promptly and at good values, but they also recognize and meet the libraries' obligations to the vendors who serve them. In all their interactions with vendors, good managers try to be fair and objective and act ethically.

Recommended Reading

Bertot, John Carlo, and Denise M. Davis, eds. *Planning and Evaluating Library Networked Services and Resources.* Westport, CT: Libraries Unlimited, 2004.

Chan, Lois Mai. *Cataloging and Classification: An Introduction.* 3rd ed. Lanham, MD: Scarecrow Press, 2007.

Evans, G. Edward, et al. "Distributors and Vendors." In *Introduction to Technical Services,* 7th ed., 181–208. Westport, CT: Libraries Unlimited, 2002.

Hsieh-Yee, Ingrid. *Organizing Audiovisual and Electronic Resources for Access: A Cataloging Guide.* 2nd ed. Westport, CT: Libraries Unlimited, 2006.

Intner, Sheila S., and Jean Weihs. *Standard Cataloging for School and Public Libraries.* 4th ed. Westport, CT: Libraries Unlimited, 2007.

Newberg, Pamela J., and Jennifer Allen. "Vendors of Cataloging for Children's Materials." In *Cataloging Correctly for Kids: An Introduction to the Tools,* 4th ed., edited by Sheila S. Intner et al., 108–13. Chicago: American Library Association, 2006.

Newberg, Pamela J., and Judith Yurczyk. "Automating the Children's Catalog." In *Cataloging Correctly for Kids: An Introduction to the Tools,* 4th ed., edited by Sheila S. Intner et al., 102–7. Chicago: American Library Association, 2006.

Pace, Andrew K. *The Ultimate Digital Library: Where the New Information Players Meet.* Chicago: American Library Association, 2003.

Taylor, Arlene G. *Introduction to Cataloging and Classification.* 10th ed. Westport, CT: Libraries Unlimited, 2006.

Notes

1. Classification done at the Library of Congress as part of Cataloging-in-Publication permits vendors to determine whether a title meets a particular customer's desired subject criteria, known as its profile.

2. *Anglo-American Cataloguing Rules,* 2nd ed., 2005 revision (Chicago: ALA; Ottawa: CLA; London: CILIP, 2005).

3. Available online as part of *Cataloger's Desktop,* from LC's Cataloging Distribution Service, http://www.loc.gov/cds/.

4. ALCTS has two: the Cataloging and Classification Section's Committee on Cataloging: Description and Access, which oversees AACR2, and the Subject Analysis Committee, which has subcommittees and task forces that oversee various aspects of subject heading lists, thesauri, and classification systems.

CHAPTER 5

Staffing the Department

◇ Recruiting Staff for Technical Services
◇ Training
◇ Directing and Supervising Staff Members
◇ Evaluating Personnel
◇ Summary

BEFORE COMPUTERIZED bibliographic networking, technical services departments had many employees at all staff levels, from senior librarians to clerks, with many levels between. Then, librarians tended to hold positions as department managers, unit supervisors, and catalogers; paraprofessionals acted as assistant supervisors, revisers, and copy catalogers (using LC cards and, later, Cataloging-in-Publication [CIP] as sources for cataloging copy); and clerks served as typists, filers, book order clerks, serials clerks, bindery clerks, and the like. After bibliographic files were automated, the number of employees fell radically, in part because computers increased individual productivity so that fewer people could accomplish as much or more work and in part because fewer tasks needed to be done. For example, preorder searching now serves to establish an order record and a preliminary catalog record as well as to identify a title for ordering purposes, whereas once it was merely the first of three separate procedures done in two different units.

In spite of the many changes that caused technical services departments to shrink and altered the balance among staff of various kinds, some things remain the same. Usually professional librarians are still hired to manage the department and do original cataloging; paraprofessionals still serve as assistant managers and do copy cataloging, although the cataloging sources and procedures are different; clerks still do the clerical work, although they may be called administrative assistants. But there are important differences: paraprofessionals often serve as unit supervisors; units are too small to need assistant supervisors; a few professional catalogers (sometimes no one other than the unit supervisor, who doubles as a cataloger) and several paraprofessional or clerical copy catalogers do all the in-house cataloging; filers and revisers are gone; and computer operators have replaced typists.

Senior librarians working in twenty-first-century technical services departments are invariably assigned management tasks. The following e-mail message, received in August 2006, describes the current assignments of a middle manager/subunit supervisor in technical services at a large university library:

> My eyeballs are a whirlin' around in my head. It has been a fun day of researching and emailing them [who know] THINGS I need to know about purchasing of catalog records for our current titles. AND, I've been working on reconciling and rewriting another draft of the "evaluation" section of the library bylaws. We have never had bylaws before in the library. Tomorrow, I . . . begin working on reshuffling and reassigning job duties of the department paraprofessionals in anticipation of the retirement of one LTA, hiring her replacement and getting another LTA assigned to the department. AND soon we begin the process of reviewing resumes to replace our division head who just retired. So far, only 3 people have applied. It may be a very select group. I would really like just to catalog one of these days. We are also preparing for a T[echnical] Services work flow review which is to take place Aug. 28-29. It is being done by a consultant hired by [the network]. We applied for a grant to do so. I am going to revive myself with a little cataloging now for an hour.[1]

Over the last several decades, when technical services department staff members have retired, moved to positions in other departments, or left the library's employ for other jobs, the vacancies have often gone unfilled. This method of eliminating staff positions is called downsizing by attrition. Employees are not fired, but the relationships and balance among the remaining workers and their job descriptions are ignored. Dislocations often occur and must be addressed by the department manager. Even when new vacancies can be filled, managers should take the opportunity to rethink work flow and reorganize where necessary.

In spite of downsizing or, sometimes, after too much of it leaves a department unable to function properly, opportunities present themselves for recruiting new people to the department. This chapter covers the basic processes of recruiting, training, directing and supervising, and evaluating staff in the technical services department.

Recruiting Staff for Technical Services

Technical services managers might or might not be involved directly in recruiting staff for their departments, depending on the hiring policies and practices of their libraries. At most, they play a leadership role in writing job descriptions, soliciting applications, evaluating candidates, and selecting those who receive job offers. At the least, managers submit authorized requests to a personnel office to hire someone and, eventually, are presented with a newly hired employee. When managers face the latter scenario it is unfortunate because their lack of input can result in having to accept and work with persons who lack requisite knowledge and skills or are otherwise difficult to integrate into the departmental workforce. Department managers should make every effort to be part of the recruitment process, leading it if they can or participating to the greatest extent possible if they cannot.

Job Descriptions and Job Titles

Before recruiting begins, working within the constraints of the library's and its parent institution's personnel policies, managers should review the department's work flow and current deployment of personnel with a view toward making changes that increase efficiency and improve

S teps you can take to do better recruiting for technical services librarians:

1. Design good jobs.
2. Do not ask for more credentials and experience than a job requires.
3. Build a recruiting network.
4. Look beyond home base.
5. Identify categories of people you want to recruit rather than individuals.
6. Offer good salaries for the level of work in the job description.
7. Provide attractive staff services, staff development, and opportunities for advancement on a challenging career path.
8. Establish effective support systems for integrating new hires into the workplace.
9. Evaluate job candidates objectively.
10. Inform every candidate of the results of the search, not just those on the short list.
11. Earn trust by being open and honest with everyone.

Source: Adapted from Sheila S. Intner, *Interfaces: Relationships between Library Technical and Public Services* (Englewood, CO: Libraries Unlimited, 1993), 183–95.

outputs, as already mentioned. An open position provides an opportunity to give members of the existing staff desired new tasks and, possibly, to upgrade positions to reflect the new duties. If, for example, an assistant acquisitions supervisor leaves, the manager might find, upon review, that the unit does not need another assistant supervisor. Instead, reassigning complex tasks formerly done by the assistant supervisor to a senior clerk capable of doing them and combining simpler tasks formerly done by the senior clerk with those done by the assistant supervisor might be a better way to handle the work. The reassignments could warrant upgrading the senior clerk to paraprofessional status and creating a new job description for a lower-level clerk or, possibly, a part-time clerk. If the senior clerk has been in place for a long time and wants to take on more responsibility, and if the library is committed to ongoing staff development, such a reorganization seems better than merely filling the vacated position.

In any event, the first step in recruitment is to write or revise the job description for the needed position and give it an appropriate title. In some libraries, job titles are dictated by inflexible institution- or library-wide personnel policies, union contracts, or longtime traditions. If so, one must work within that framework. But if there is room for change, a new title should be considered and assigned. It should reflect the nature of the job's principal tasks and furnish a sense of purpose to the person who holds it.[2] Most important, it should not be misleading when defined in current terms. For example, an advertisement in a professional journal for a collection development librarian seen a few years ago outlined the job responsibilities of a copy cataloger, yet *catalog, cataloger,* or *cataloging* was absent from the title.

Qualifications should be geared to the principal duties of the job and not exceed them. Copy catalogers, for example, do not need a master's degree in library and information science, but they could benefit from learning about cataloging by taking a few library school courses. Catalogers who encounter foreign-language items once in a while do not need to speak the languages (they might consult a colleague or someone in another department with language expertise), but cataloging specialists dealing every day with foreign-language materials do. Each qualification that appears in a job description should be matched by a principal job duty, not a once-in-a-while task.

Salaries should be set as high as the library can afford to pay for good workers in each employment grade, not as low as administrators think they can go. (The key term here is *good workers*.) Full-time librarians

Job titles need careful consideration. At the least, a job title should bear a close relationship to the responsibilities written into its description. Sometimes, however, job title and responsibilities do not correspond. Following are examples from published advertisements.

Title	Responsibilities
Collection Specialist	Perform reference and collection maintenance duties; includes all aspects of readers' advisory services, creating thematic displays, weeding library materials, and recommending materials for collection purchase.
Technical Services Dept. Head	Responsible for administration and management of Technical Services Department and for the maintenance and development of the adult materials collection, . . . supervising the cataloging and processing, . . . and reference and readers' advisory.
Electronic Resources Librarian	Install, configure, maintain, and troubleshoot electronic equipment and systems, including computers, digital projectors, cameras, printers, scanners, bar code readers, etc. . . . Evaluate and recommend acquisition of electronic resources, . . . manage publication of library newsletter, . . . design and produce other library publications.
Coordinator of Technical Services	Oversee serials, electronic collections, and technical processes, . . . oversee metadata, coordinate digital projects.
Technical Services Information Specialist	Provide reference and research instruction to students and faculty (some classroom instruction required) and perform collection development and acquisitions activities.

Title	Responsibilities
Electronic/ Technical Services Librarian	Primary responsibility in coordinating the electronic services of the Library. . . . Primary responsibility in coordinating the technical services of the Library. . . . Regularly scheduled reference desk hours.

should earn a living wage after taxes and not have to seek added income to put food on the table. Library workers lacking the master's degree should earn as much as they would in comparable jobs elsewhere.

Building a Pool of Applicants

An ideal pool of applicants consists of enough qualified people that employers have a choice, perhaps somewhere around ten to twelve applicants. Job ads that fail to attract qualified applicants need to be revised,[3] as do ads that attract hundreds of applications. Such a large pool is likely to include many unqualified and overqualified people, and it is no bonus to have to sift through the credentials of large numbers of inappropriate applicants.

If managers are responsible for recruitment, the work can be much easier if they can call on a network of career-services contacts such as guidance counselors, educators, and job-placement officers. It takes effort to develop and maintain contacts with nearby library school, college, and high school faculty and administrators, but it can pay off handsomely. The scope of the search should match the importance of the position, going beyond local borders to statewide, regional, or nationwide solicitations when someone with special knowledge is sought. The cost of doing broader searches may be higher than those confined to a library's immediate vicinity, but the return on the investment is better applicant pools.

Evaluating the Candidates

Candidates who have appropriate qualifications and are being considered for a position should be evaluated as objectively as possible. Criteria for selecting the successful applicant should be written in detail before evaluation begins. The criteria, while linked closely to the duties in the job description, may go beyond them. Measures that will be used for each criterion should be decided in advance, and the process for determining the measures (analyzing applications, telephone or on-site interviews or both, reference checks, etc.) should be followed in the same way for each person to ensure fair treatment. Highly subjective, non-task-related factors such as personality or temperament can be considered at some point, but not before objective criteria have been exhausted. If several candidates seem to have equal merit based on the objective criteria, subjective factors can help to differentiate them.

The candidate pool is usually winnowed down to a short list of two to six candidates who are asked to participate in face-to-face interviews. In public libraries, interviews frequently are half-day or daylong events in which candidates meet with administrators and librarians both individually and in groups and with members of governing boards. In academic settings, interviews tend to be more elaborate, including meetings with individuals and groups in the department, the library, and the institution; formal presentations by the applicants; question-and-answer sessions; meals in nice local restaurants; and parties, sometimes at the manager's home. Interviews may take two or three days and involve hosting each interviewee as graciously as budgets allow. The interview is an opportunity to impress the candidates with the attractiveness of the library as well as to judge their abilities. Once the interviews are over, names on the short list (minus any that the interviews found wanting) are ranked. At this point, an offer of employment may be made to the top-ranked applicant, or a second round of interviews may be conducted for all or some of them.

Selecting the New Employee

If a fair, open process has been followed and the evaluative criteria are explicit, the most appropriate candidate should be obvious. Even if that person was not the top choice of all department members, each should understand the reason for the selection. In smaller libraries, new staff members must interact closely with everyone else. These relationships may be easier to establish if they begin with knowledge of the new person's credentials and the belief he or she earned the position. In larger libraries, an important element in building and maintaining morale is that staff members believe all personnel are treated fairly. A search in which the criteria for selection and the candidates' qualifications are a clear match can be expected to foster that belief and avoid engendering private grievances or feeding rumors that someone's favorite was selected over better-qualified applicants.

The offer of a position does not always end the search process. Negotiations over the terms of employment can ensue if the salary, benefits, and job details have not been spelled out to the candidate's satisfaction or if they were left to be determined after the offer was made. During the negotiations, good managers should know their limits of flexibility in meeting a candidate's demands and inform the library's representatives. Although many job offers are accepted without much delay, some result in protracted negotiations. Good-faith efforts must be made to work out the remaining details with the selected candidate before library representatives can conclude their offer has failed. Only when this conclusion is conveyed to the candidate is the library free to make an offer to another candidate. Attractive candidates may receive several offers at once and have trouble deciding which one to accept and under what terms.

Once the selected candidate accepts the offer of employment, plans for integrating that person into the technical services workforce—in whatever position, from manager to clerical assistant—should begin.

Training

New staff members need training even if they previously worked in the same library or the same department. If the person is new to the library, thorough introduction to the policies, practices, and traditions of the library is essential. It takes time for a new staff member to absorb it all, but giving someone a few days or weeks to learn the ropes is a good investment. New department managers who have never worked in the library before have the most to learn but are often given the least help in this regard. One way to address the problem is for new managers to spend part of each day during their first few weeks shadowing key staff members until current operations within the department are well understood and part of the day during the same period partnering with peers who head other departments until the way they operate is clear.

Effective training is made up of three elements: good trainers, well-designed training programs, and opportunities for practice. Practice, in particular, is important and should not be neglected or expected to be done on a new staff member's own time. No one performs at optimal levels immediately after learning how to do something new. People need time to repeat and experiment with what they have learned, discover the variations inherent in the task or process, and make and correct errors in the way they do it before becoming adept. The learning curve will vary with each person as well as with each new task or process, but rarely is demonstrating how something should be done enough to teach it to another person. In order to master a task, the trainee must do it with guidance, do it alone, practice it, then use the newly acquired skills on a regular basis.

Just because a staff member can perform a task does not mean he or she can teach it. One can learn to be a good teacher, but some people seem to have a knack for it. With time and effort, these people can become outstanding trainers. Good managers ought to have the ability to teach because staff training is often part of their job descriptions, but if they lack that ability they should recognize it and find others within the department who have the necessary skills.

The Library of Congress (LC) and the Association for Library Collections and Technical Services (ALCTS, formerly Resources and Technical Services Division [RTSD]) led the training of catalogers and other technical services librarians in how to train. Focused efforts go back to a series of two-day workshops on AACR2 held in anticipation of its implementation on January 1, 1980. The Library of Congress's senior catalogers explained AACR policies that became standard for all U.S. libraries. Participants went home and trained their staffs. State library organizations continued the effort, as did RTSD.* In the mid-1980s, to help ensure the quality of its shared cataloging database, OCLC's PACNET ran workshops titled "Quick and Easy Cataloging" to introduce standards to copy catalogers who lacked library training. Soon after, the need to train catalogers in the art of training was so critical that LC wrote a full script, the *Train the Trainer Manual,* based on the way it trained its own staff. The manual included everything needed to conduct an on-the-job training program, including icebreakers, exercises, examples and illustrations, evaluation sheets, and full scripts of lectures. It could be purchased in versions for instructors and students. Independently field-tested, the manual proved effective.† Currently, LC, ALCTS, and the Program for Cooperative Cataloging are focusing on metadata and other new tools needed for digital collections.‡

---

* RTSD/ALCTS continued mounting regional workshops as well as participating in joint efforts with LC and the bibliographic networks. An example of a statewide effort was the Minnesota AACR2 trainers, who not only gave workshops but also participated in the publication of numerous cataloging manuals.

† Sheila S. Intner, "A Field Test of the Library of Congress's *Training the Trainer Course,*" *Education for Information* (September 1991): 225–47.

‡ At this writing, a set of courses titled "Cataloging for the 21st Century" is under development.

Training involves developing support materials. These may take a variety of forms, from cheat sheets or quick reference guides that outline the basic steps of a task to elaborate training manuals. Instead of hastily scrawled, ad hoc instructions that might or might not include all the information a trainee needs, properly written guides that have been tested with real trainees and found to be complete and effective are worth the effort of word processing and printing. Putting training materials into a database makes them easier to revise and update, customize for particular tasks or individuals, and distribute as needed. Tutorials and other kinds of practice materials should be available for trainees to use following training sessions. Most of all, new skills need to be used on the job without delay to ensure they are not forgotten before they are needed.

Directing and Supervising Staff Members

Part of a department manager's job is telling staff members what work to do and overseeing that they do it properly while simultaneously allowing them to have control over their jobs and respecting their special knowledge. This makes the tasks of directing and supervising staff sound like walking a tightrope and, to some extent, it is, although it was not always the case. In the past, libraries functioned in a strict hierarchical style in which supervisors told staff what to do and later decided, unilaterally, how well it was done. In twenty-first-century libraries, this style is generally unacceptable. Librarians recognize the importance of enabling staff members to take satisfaction in their work and valuing each individual's personal contributions.

Some managers keep a balance between manager-directed and staff-directed assignments by creating teams responsible for making and evaluating work assignments. What must be kept in mind, however, is that managers have the ultimate responsibility for the work done in their departments, even if they delegate the tasks of assigning and supervising it to a team.

Individual style and the current management style of the library usually govern how likely a manager is to assign work to individuals directly or to a team that will decide how to get it done or some of each. Given the variation in the kinds of work done in today's technical services departments and the different kinds of staff members doing the work, good managers will do some of each. The amount of managerial control can be linked to the knowledge, experience, and histories of the people doing the work. Experienced, credentialed librarians who have demonstrated their competence in doing tasks such as original cataloging or book conservation can be self-directed. Less experienced, less knowledgeable people without track records need more direction and closer supervision. In large libraries, direction and supervision may be delegated to a unit supervisor but should still be monitored on a regular basis by the department manager, who, as mentioned, is ultimately responsible.

Supervision should not be neglected or relegated to a casual question such as "How are things going?" every so often. Benchmarks should be set by the department manager and the team leader, unit supervisor, or self-directed staff member, as appropriate, and routinely checked—weekly, monthly, or quarterly, depending on the activities and the personnel involved. Some staff members will alert supervisors immediately when a problem occurs; others will not. Interim reports not only make end-of-the-year evaluation easier but also forestall ugly surprises. Regular monitoring does not prevent bad things from

According to Peggy Johnson, leaders have a particularly strong need to communicate effectively. Leaders must develop the following characteristics to help create an environment in which understanding and clarity thrive:

- Trust
- Empathy
- Openness
- Intuition

Source: Peggy Johnson, "The Role of Empathy in Managerial Communication," in *Library Communication: The Language of Leadership*, ed. Donald E. Riggs (Chicago: American Library Association, 1991), 78–87.

happening, but it ensures that when problems occur, they do not go on for very long without being discovered and addressed.

Evaluating Personnel

Staff evaluation is an important task for department managers. It should not be delegated to others unless the staff is very large and managers cannot handle the job alone. In that event, managers can enlist the help of unit supervisors, who can be asked to gather information for people in their units and organize it appropriately. Even so, managers should prepare the final interpretations using the data provided.

Evaluations usually are done once a year. Ideally, the process should be as objective as possible, examining the work done, not the person, except in unusual circumstances (for example, if the employee has special needs that must be taken into account). One way to achieve objectivity is to use a process similar to the following:

1. Write measurable objectives for each person being evaluated. (This part should be done before the evaluation period starts.)
2. Gather data measuring the work done.
3. Compare the stated objectives and the completed work.
4. Interpret the results.

All parts should be done in writing and become part of the employee's record.

Interpretations sometimes are questioned, especially if they show poor performance. Managers need to be prepared to deal with all kinds of results as well as all kinds of reactions. Good managers do all they can to avoid bias in interpreting the results. One way to avoid bias is to be open about all parts of the process and to allow employees unhappy with their manager's reports to prepare their own reports that explain or challenge the manager's interpretations and that are added to the record.

It helps to have staff-evaluation forms for recording the objectives, the data, and the results of each evaluation. Well-run libraries provide forms for this purpose, but if none are available, good managers should design their own. It is imperative that employees understand—before they begin the evaluation period—how their work is being evaluated, what data will be used in the process, and how excellent, good, fair, and poor levels of performance are defined. Managers who keep employees informed, conduct open processes, and interpret results without bias are being fair and honest.

Summary

This chapter has covered the tasks of recruiting and helping to hire staff, training them, supervising them, and evaluating their performance. These tasks inevitably involve encountering and dealing with the differing strengths, weaknesses, and personal styles of the individuals who work in the department. A good manager cultivates qualities of patience, tolerance, diplomacy, and flexibility to do these tasks well. The department manager serves as the role model for the staff, even though being a model is rarely listed in a job description. When stresses occur, as they inevitably do, it is up to the manager to be the buffer, deflecting or absorbing the impact on the department. Like a parent, the manager is responsible for developing a staff that gets along and works well together, and the manager takes the blame when they do not.

I n a survey report titled "Emerging Issues in Academic Library Cataloging and Technical Services," researchers for Primary Research Group, who interviewed cataloging or technical services managers at nine academic libraries of varying sizes located in different regions of the United States, found that none had specific cataloging quotas. Some respondents said they had specified task times associated with particular materials. Some also indicated that individual catalogers with productivity problems were asked to set personal benchmarks to demonstrate improvement.

Source: Announcement in Online Audiovisual Catalogers electronic discussion list, April 13, 2007. The report, ISBN 1-574440-086-X, can be purchased from Primary Research Group, http://www.primaryresearch.com.

Part of the manager's job is creating an environment in which staff members can do their jobs effectively. This is not always easy. Conflicts sometimes arise, and rivalries can develop between individuals or between units in the department. Staff members become ill or suffer other crises. Larger staffing issues in the library sometimes benefit and other times penalize department staff. The department manager must be ready to resolve problems as they occur and, at the same time, do all that can be done to ensure that productivity remains strong.

It is not easy to maintain strong morale among department members and to achieve consistently high levels of performance, but it is very important. It takes effort to exercise authority without being authoritarian and to take responsibility without usurping individual pride or squelching continuing growth. Good managers must try to foster an atmosphere of trust from which everyone can draw strength and satisfaction.

Recommended Reading

Avery, Elizabeth Fuseler, et al., eds. *Staff Development: A Practical Guide.* 3rd ed. Chicago: American Library Association, 2001.

Bazirjian, Rosann, and Nancy Markle Stanley. "Assessing the Effectiveness of Team-Based Structures in Libraries." *Library Collections, Acquisitions, and Technical Services* 25 (Summer 2001): 131–57.

Cohn, John M., and Ann L. Kelsey. *Staffing the Modern Library: A How-to-Do-It Manual.* New York: Neal-Schuman, 2005.

Eden, Bradford Lee, ed. *Innovative Redesign and Reorganization of Library Technical Services: Paths for the Future and Case Studies.* Westport, CT: Libraries Unlimited, 2004.

Evans, G. Edward. *Performance Management and Appraisal: A How-to-Do-It Manual for Librarians.* New York: Neal-Schuman, 2004.

Evans, G. Edward, et al. "Staffing." Chap. 2 in *Introduction to Technical Services,* 7th ed. Westport, CT: Libraries Unlimited, 2002.

Hill, Janet Swan. *Education for Cataloging and the Organization of Information: Pitfalls and the Pendulum.* New York: Haworth Information Press, 2002.

Intner, Sheila S. "The Good Professional." *American Libraries* 29 (March 1998): 48–50.

Mayo, Diane, and Jeanne Goodrich, eds. *Staffing for Results: A Guide to Working Smarter.* Chicago: Public Library Association, 2002.

McLaren, Mary. "Team Structure: Establishment and Evolution within Technical Services at the University of Kentucky Libraries." *Library Cataloging, Acquisitions, and Technical Services* 25 (Winter 2001): 357–69.

Recruitment, Retention, and Restructuring: Human Resources in Academic Libraries. Chicago: Association of College and Research Libraries, 2006.

Sanchez, Elaine. *Emerging Issues in Academic Library Cataloging and Technical Services.* New York: Primary Research Group, 2007.

Simmons-Welburn, Janice, and Beth McNeil, eds. *Human Resource Management in Today's Academic Library: Meeting Challenges and Creating Opportunities.* Westport, CT: Libraries Unlimited, 2004.

Smith, Glenda. "Aiming for Continuous Improvement: Performance Measurement in a Re-engineered Technical Services." *Library Collections, Acquisitions, and Technical Services* 25 (Spring 2001): 81–92.

Strasner, Teresa. "Continuing Education Needs for Technical Services Paraprofessionals in Academic Libraries." *Colorado Libraries* 26 (Spring 2000): 2–4.

Wilder, Stanley J. "Demographic Trends Affecting Professional Technical Services Staffing in ARL Libraries." *Cataloging and Classification Quarterly* 34, nos. 1 and 2 (2002): 53–57.

Notes

1. Message reproduced with the sender's permission; received by the author August 1, 2006, from a colleague.

2. Job titles and professional naming can have subtle effects on employees. For a discussion of this issue, see Sheila S. Intner, "The Technical Services Mystique," in *Interfaces: Relationships between Library Technical and Public Services* (Englewood, CO: Libraries Unlimited, 1993): 3–9.

3. D. Whitney Coe relates an incident illustrating this point in "Recruitment: A Positive Process," in *Recruiting, Educating, and Training Cataloging Librarians: Solving the Problems,* ed. Sheila S. Intner and Janet Swan Hill, 53–72 (Westport, CT: Greenwood Press, 1989).

CHAPTER 6

Budgeting and Finance

✧ Planning the Departmental Budget
✧ Tracking the Departmental Budget
✧ Reporting
✧ Summary

TWO KINDS of tasks govern the finances of the technical services department: the preliminary tasks of planning and preparing the departmental budget and getting it approved and the postapproval tasks of supervising the approved budget over the budget cycle (usually a year) and reporting on all department income and expenditures at the end of the cycle. Responsibility for preparing draft budgets and obtaining approval for them is not always included in the department manager's job description, but supervising the approved budget is.

Understanding the library's financial operations is essential in the preliminary phase of budget preparation as well as in doing a good job of supervising department finances and reporting at the end of the budget cycle. This chapter covers both kinds of tasks. Managers who do not plan, prepare, and gain approval for budgets might gain some useful insight from the first part of the chapter, but, if they prefer, they can skip that section and go directly to the sections on supervising expenditures and reporting the results at the end of the budget cycle.

Planning the Departmental Budget

Libraries use standard methods and forms to allocate available funds for different types of costs, such as personnel, equipment, and supplies. Together, these allocations make up a budget covering a specified

A public library director decided to share some of his authority over funding and asked each of his department heads to prepare a departmental budget for the next year. Until then, the director had done all the budgeting alone, tracking down costs, juggling numbers, and figuring costs for different mixes of services, staffing, and programs. The request came out of the blue, but the department heads went to work on the task. When they met, the budgets were the main topic of discussion. W—the head of reference—was unusually silent during the discussion, until a colleague turned to her and asked, "How is your budget shaping up, W?" "I'm not submitting one," W replied. A hubbub ensued as her colleagues all exclaimed, "But you have to!" "What do you mean, you aren't submitting one?" "How can you do that!" "Are you serious?" "What will he say?" "How are you going to get away with it?" W smiled a little Cheshire cat smile and continued, "Every year I get all the money I want. I get all the staff and all the materials I request. I have no reason to put figures on paper, and if I do I might not get everything, so I've decided not to submit a budget." The deadline came. Every department head except W gave a budget to the director. Weeks later, when the director presented his final budget to the library board, the department heads met again and compared notes: children's received more than requested; technical services, youth, adult services, readers' advisory, music, public relations, maintenance, and circulation received all they requested; but reference received the same budget as the previous year, which was tantamount to a significant cut. A few months later, W resigned.

period of time, usually a year. The budget cycle, called the fiscal year, may or may not coincide with the calendar year. Managers need to know what period their library's fiscal year covers. Schools often use July 1 to June 30 as their fiscal year, and public libraries usually coordinate their fiscal year to match the one used by the community government. New budgets are presented, approved, and implemented on a regular schedule, sometimes more than one year in advance.

Planners consider three budget cycles simultaneously: the previous cycle, the current cycle, and the forthcoming cycle. Individual institutions have their own rules about such issues as moving funds from one budget line to another within a budget period and how unspent funds or shortfalls, if there are any, are handled at the end of the budget period, but their budgets tend to look very much alike and cover the same cost factors. The line-item format is popular. It divides a total budget into a series of lines, each representing a cost factor (personnel, equipment, supplies, etc.). Within the limits of the library's total budget for each line, individual departments receive whatever portion is allocated to them. When a department's allocations for all the lines are combined, the total is the departmental budget.

Library finance officers can allocate the same percentage of every budget line to a department, a practice called across-the-board allocation. The key decision is what percentage each department is to receive. For example, the technical services department might be allocated 20 percent of the library budget, which means that technical services will get 20 percent of the personnel budget, 20 percent of the equipment budget, and so forth. Alternatively, decision makers can allocate different percentages depending on the nature of the budget category. In that case, the technical services department might get 20 percent of the personnel line, 30 percent of the equipment line, 15 percent of the supplies line, and so on. Often, library finance officers request that proposed budgets be submitted annually from every department. Then they go to work trying to balance the requests against available funds in a way they believe best serves library-wide goals.

Forecasting

Good planning depends on accurate estimates of what things will cost in the future. Budgets based on current costs might or might not cover the same level of operations in the next budget cycle, depending on whether individual costs will rise, fall, or remain the same. If operations remain the same but all costs rise, the budget will not stretch to cover them. If all costs fall, a portion will remain unspent. If some costs rise and others fall, the outcome will be based on the eventual totals—the bottom line—which could turn out to be either a shortfall or a surplus.

Budget planners forecast two things: the expected level of operations and the future price for each cost factor. Gathering information about how important cost categories may change in the future is key to deciding what dollar allocations to use in budget plans. Some information is available from the popular library press, such as *American Libraries* and *Library Journal;* trade publications in related fields like computing, publishing, and education (for example, *D-Lib Magazine, Publisher's Weekly, Education Week*); online discussion lists, and the popular press.[1] Personnel costs are surveyed and published annually, and publications such as the *Bowker Annual* cover matters that affect costs directly or indirectly.

Common sense dictates that even if operations remain the same, budgets must increase when costs increase. Otherwise, operations must decrease or change in some other way that lowers costs to meet the limitations imposed by the budget. Experience in recent decades suggests that costs increase faster than library budgets, while public expectations regarding library materials and services continue to rise. Librarians have had to do more with less as well as try to develop new sources of income to balance the shortfalls this situation inevitably produces.

In the last quarter of the twentieth century, computers helped librarians produce more work with fewer staff members. The cost of computerizing catalogs and other library data was high but was often funded by grants and other outside sources. As already mentioned, technical services departments shrank and reorganized after computerization. In the twenty-first century, changes driven by technology continue to occur, but their effects on departmental budgets are not as dramatic and, because the change process is becoming familiar, are a little easier to predict.

Budget Preparation

Preparing the budget involves taking the template used by the library's or institution's financial office and filling in the amounts needed to operate the technical services department for the next budget cycle. If it is a line-item budget, each line must contain the amount needed for that cost factor. The template will probably include, but will not be limited to, the following categories:

1. *Personnel:* generally the largest amount; divided into salaries and benefits, with benefits figured as a percentage of salary; may also include allocations for staff development, including professional association dues, conference registrations, work-related travel, workshops, professional materials, and the like

2. *Equipment:* may or may not include the cost of computers; generally includes copy machines (whether owned or rented); equipment used for spine labeling, binding, and repairs; and any other equipment used in the department

3. *Maintenance:* often computed as an increasing percentage of the cost of equipment that requires ongoing maintenance and may include the cost of service contracts if that cost does not appear elsewhere

4. *Supplies:* includes office supplies such as paper, envelopes, pens and pencils, paper clips, rubber bands, and mailing labels and technical supplies such as binding and repair materials, spine labels, and bar codes

5. *Postage:* may be figured as a percentage of total library postage costs

6. *Telephone service:* may be figured as a percentage of total library telephone service costs

7. *Contract/consulting services:* may include cost of bibliographic network membership and services, vendor services, and outside trainers, temporary catalogers, inputters, consultants, and so forth

Line-Item Budget

101	Staff	$250,000
102	Contractual (includes OCLC)	75,000
103	Supplies	50,000
104	Equipment	100,000
105	Telephone	25,000
106	Miscellaneous	25,000
Total		$525,000

Departmental Budget

BI	$75,000
Circulation	50,000
Information desk/reference	200,000
Technical services	75,000
Collection development	50,000
Document delivery (includes ILL)	75,000
Total	$525,000

Figure 6.1   Typical library budgets

8. *Overhead:* figured as a factor of the total of other costs, usually set by the library or the library's parent institution

Figure 6.1 shows a typical library budget.

Trade-offs

Some cost factors are related, in which case a change in one affects the others. For example, buying more vendor services (such as outsourcing cataloging) reduces the work done in-house by department staff and the associated costs, but it raises the total cost of contract services. Similarly, increasing the per-order quantities of important supplies (bar codes, spine labels, etc.) reduces their per-piece costs but means spending more money at the time the purchases are made. Such trade-offs should be reconsidered each time a new budget is planned to see if changing buying habits can save money for the library.

Budget planners should also consider steps that might be taken to streamline operations. Good department managers do not wait for library administrators to tell them about cost-cutting possibilities; they have already thought of them and incorporated feasible ideas into their budget plans.

Price versus Value

An old adage scolds the person who knows the price of everything and the value of nothing. For instance, the price of full catalog records with authority control from source A might be higher than uncontrolled, minimal-level records from source B, but buying better cataloging might result in fewer search failures and reduce the number of times patrons need help from reference librarians. Overall, source A might be the better choice. Budget planners should be concerned about total value received from dollars spent and be able to explain it clearly when asked.

A problem facing technical services budget planners is the difficulty of putting prices on quality and speed, things highly prized in department outputs, or on patron satisfaction, which department outputs are supposed to address. How much is it worth to obtain patron-wanted materials a week earlier than usual? Are library patrons more satisfied when their requested materials arrive that quickly and, if so, how much more? Does it make a noticeable difference? Before paying higher prices, technical services managers should be certain the answer to the last question is yes, not only to librarians but also to the public. Relative terms such as *fast, high quality,* and even *more satisfied* can be translated into measurable terms so the value of expenditures can be computed. Some kinds of value are easier to determine: for example, assigning a dollar figure to a book's postrepair circulation can measure the value of repairing the library's older books.

Relative terms such as *fast* and *slow* or *good* and *bad* are interpreted subjectively and can mean different things to different people. To be useful in professional practice, they should be translated into objective measures on which everyone can agree, such as the following:

Fast = not more than x working days (x = an agreed-upon average number of working days)

Slow = more than x working days (x = an agreed-upon average number of working days)

Example: An acquisitions unit and its book wholesaler agree that 5 working days is acceptable for the wholesaler to deliver in-print U.S. trade books and that 10 working days is acceptable for in-print books published abroad. If, on average, the wholesaler delivers 1,000 in-print books ordered by the library in fewer than 5 working days for U.S. trade books and 10 working days for books published elsewhere, the library is getting "fast" service. Individual deliveries may exceed the averages, but overall performance must equal the averages or fall below them.

Good = meets a standard or test(s) of quality

Bad = does not meet a standard or test(s) of quality

Example: "Good cataloging" is defined as meeting or exceeding the Program for Cooperative Cataloging core record standard and having no errors that affect retrieval. "Bad cataloging" is defined as containing less information than the core record standard or containing any errors that affect retrieval.

Approving the Budget

Preparing budget plans for the next cycle and presenting them to library directors is rarely the end of the process. In one approach to budgeting, the technical services budget plan may be combined with those from other library departments and presented as a package by the director to the library's funding body. In such cases, the library budget request competes with requests from other community or institutional units for available funds. The director is expected to defend the library budget plan successfully. When budgets are finally approved and funds are distributed, the library might get what it requested or not. When a lower total is approved, someone, usually the library director or management team, decides how to deal with the shortfall: divide it equally among all departments (across-the-board cuts); divide it unequally but take some funds from every department; or divide it unequally but take funds from some departments and not from others. Once a budget receives final approval, the department manager usually must make do with whatever the department receives.

In another approach to budgeting, the director knows the total funds approved for the library. The technical services budget plan competes with those of other departments, and the director can either approve it as submitted or approve a lower amount. Depending on personal managerial style, the director might ask department managers to defend their budget plans either separately or together in a budget-approval meeting. Either way, a wise technical services manager will not only have all the facts and figures at hand to defend each budget expense but stand ready to explain clearly how spending the requested funds advances the library's overall goals and objectives. Relating department activities to overall goals and objectives is crucial to success.

Tracking the Departmental Budget

Department managers are nearly always charged with overseeing the budget throughout the budget cycle by monitoring expenditures and making sure funds are spent appropriately but not overspent.

If managers have prepared their department's budget and done the work connected with its preparation, they already are familiar with allocations and how they were computed. If not, their first step in tracking the departmental budget is to become thoroughly familiar with the amounts assigned to each budget category (that is, each budget line) as well as with the assumptions and estimates underlying the numbers. Then they can supervise expenditures knowledgeably.

The manager should be aware of when payments of various kinds occur—daily, weekly, monthly, or irregularly—and check them all periodically, though not necessarily each time a payment is made. Requiring managerial approval before paying bills slows down the payment process unnecessarily. It is better for the manager to check on payments periodically, perhaps weekly or monthly. When orders for equipment and supplies are placed, managers should know in advance how much money is committed and keep track of these commitments the same way acquisitions librarians encumber funds when ordering materials. Money to pay for ongoing expenses such as bibliographic network services, subscription services, and approval plans should be earmarked at the start of the budget cycle so they are not mistakenly viewed as free funds available to be spent on other things.

Sometimes budgets include discretionary funds that department managers can use for unspecified purposes, generally to address unforeseen gaps that can crop up during the cycle. If there is no budget line for professional development, managers might use discretionary funds to send staff members to workshops, hire professional trainers, or buy educational materials. Discretionary funds might be used to set up a book-repair unit in a library that has none or to hire a consultant to address preservation problems. Or they might be used to conduct an experiment of buying a different mix of vendor services to see if the results warrant a permanent change. It is particularly important that expenditures of discretionary funds be properly documented and tracked because managers are directly accountable for them.

Similarly, if a department employee leaves before the end of the budget cycle and the funds for his or her salary-benefit package are not

Overseeing a budget is an important responsibility that should be spelled out for managers new to the task. Losing track of small charges, in particular, can prove disastrous, as happened to one young librarian. She was the newly appointed manager of a branch of a well-funded city library. In January, during her first week on the job, she was told her branch was allotted X dollars for materials. Excited about the generous amount of money she had to spend, she immediately began ordering titles she knew her patrons would enjoy. Every week, issues of review journals were routed to her, and she checked off numerous selections for her branch. April arrived and with it came a new task: submission of a quarterly report for the branch. This included, in addition to the numbers of patron visits, materials circulated, programs held, and so forth during the first three months of the year, a count of staff hours and expenditures. The branch head compiled her statistics and waited for a report from the acquisitions department that totaled the encumbrances for her orders. When it came and she saw the amount, she discovered to her horror that she had spent the entire materials budget for the year. She learned the hard way that even big budgets evaporate quickly when a manager fails to count up small expenditures and loses track of the bottom line. Her mistake was costly for the branch also. Her director allowed her to spend a little against the next year's allotments, but as the months passed, patrons found fewer and fewer new titles, which gave them the erroneous impression that other branches had better resources.

going to be spent, or if a product or service drops in price and its entire allotment is not going to be spent, the manager should account for what happens to the resulting surplus funds. When library rules permit taking money from one budget line and using it to pay for expenses on a different line, managers can use the savings the way they think best.

If not, managers can petition administrators for permission to use the savings to fund worthwhile projects in different lines.

The easiest way to track an approved budget is to set it up as a spreadsheet in which four columns are defined for each line: the original allocation, earmarked expenses, actual expenditures, and current uncommitted balance. Weekly or monthly, as the manager checks each type of expenditure, the figures in the columns can be updated and new totals automatically computed. This way, unforeseen expenses or new commitments can quickly be brought into the picture, and the end results can be understood immediately. What managers want to avoid is discovering at the end of the budget cycle that unrecognized expenses ate up whatever cushions were built into the budget (such as discretionary funds) and caused the department to overspend budget limits.

Typically, library administrators check periodically throughout the year to determine what is happening to department finances. They expect updates on department spending at specified times, not only at the end of the year. They probably are reporting to library governing bodies and want to avoid ugly surprises when it is too late to make adjustments. Changes to approved budgets can occur during the budget cycle for many reasons, including failure to receive expected operating funds or to generate expected income from endowments, grants, or fund-raising. Although it is frustrating and difficult, managers may be notified of cuts long after the cycle has started. When this happens, cuts must be instituted immediately, sometimes halting department activity in its tracks. Saddest of all are extensive cuts that can only be addressed by letting staff members go or forgoing important activities.

Also frustrating but somewhat less aggravating are sudden windfalls at the end of a budget cycle that must be spent right away or be lost. Wise managers are prepared for such occurrences with projects and orders that consume the money without delay. They seize the opportunity to order larger volumes of consumable supplies, buy a new computerized labeling system, or hire a consultant to help prepare a library disaster plan. Good relations with peers can help managers avoid problems in technical services when, for instance, end-of-the-year windfalls prompt the reference department to request new databases or the children's department to ask for replacements for all the library's worn picture books. Nothing substitutes for being prepared to respond to positive financial changes, even if they do not happen very often.

Reporting

Reporting the department's financial results at the end of a budget cycle is an important responsibility of the department manager. Managers who keep good records throughout the cycle will have the data they need to prepare reports explaining how the department spent its money.

Some large amounts may not require much explanation. For instance, if allocations for staffing covered current personnel at current pay scales, they are totally consumed if no staff members leave their positions, no new people are hired, and salary-benefit packages do not change. The same can be said for other cost categories, provided forecasts are accurate and nothing changes.

Managers cannot close out budgets for a fiscal year on the day it ends. All commitments made during the cycle may not be complete and the bills may not be paid until after the date passes. Goods and services ordered before the old cycle ends are still charged to the department, even though they have not been delivered and payments will not be made until later. Usually library or institutional policies define a postcycle grace period that may last for weeks or months. After the grace period ends, the payment of outstanding bills can no longer be applied to the old cycle and must be charged against the new one. Wise managers can avoid overlap problems by specifying that financial commitments will be automatically canceled if goods or services are not delivered by a designated date. Vendors who accept orders with such qualifications should be clearly told they must meet delivery dates or lose the orders.

End-of-cycle reports should include at least the following:

1. Tables or spreadsheets showing budget allocations, amounts expended, and net balances; an added column showing the percentage of the budget represented by each allocation or actual expenditure is useful also
2. Explanations for unusual expenses or expenses not included in the approved budget
3. Explanations of funds moved from one line to another, if present, with acknowledgment of special approvals, if given
4. Rationales for over- or underspending

The report should begin with a budget narrative that describes, in general terms, the highlights of the financial cycle. In the narrative, forecasts that turned out to be especially high or low, unforeseen events that had financial repercussions, and changes made to allocations should be discussed. Examples of things that bear special mention include the unexpected loss or addition of personnel, changes in salaries or benefits, changes in the prices of important services or supplies, initiation of new or different operations or procedures, exceptional projects that prompted unusual purchases, and the like. The budget narrative should be followed by tables and charts that document the budget as a whole and specific components that merit mention. A brief summary of department activities might be added, especially if managers do not also submit separate annual reports.

Summary

Some managers of technical services departments are responsible for preparing and obtaining approval for their department's budget as well as for monitoring it and reporting on the results at the end of the budget cycle, whereas other managers are responsible only for monitoring and reporting. For those who must do the entire job of managing finances, understanding the way the library and its parent institution or community do things and using the same model is important. Knowing how planned expenditures can help the library meet its goals and objectives is important also and can be helpful in getting the draft budget approved. Being open to new ways of operating that can save money or increase quality or both should be high on the manager's list every time she or he prepares a new budget plan.

For managers who only need to supervise budgets and report on them after the budget cycle has ended, the main tasks are watching payments (which may mean being sure those who handle the payments report back regularly) and maintaining good records, preferably in the form of online spreadsheets. Updating fund balances is an ongoing requirement that can be delegated, but checking the balances frequently enough that problems are detected before they become crises is something the manager should do personally.

Writing reports at the end of the budget cycle that explain how the department's money was spent involves providing tables that show the numbers budget line by budget line and an accompanying narrative that explains, in general terms, what happened with various funds during the year. Unusual or unexpected expenses should be mentioned and explained in greater detail, as should discretionary funds. In particular need of explanation are budget lines that were over- or underspent. If no other reporting is done at the end of the cycle, a summary of departmental operations can be added to the budget report.

Recommended Reading

Daubert, Madeline J. *Financial Management for Small and Medium-Sized Libraries.* Chicago: American Library Association, 1993.

Hall-Ellis, Sylvia D., and Frank W. Hoffmann. *Grantsmanship for Small Libraries and School Library Media Centers.* Englewood, CO: Libraries Unlimited, 1999.

Martin, Murray S. *Academic Library Budgets.* Greenwich, CT: JAI Press, 1993.

———. *Collection Development and Finance: A Guide to Strategic Library-Materials Budgeting.* Chicago: American Library Association, 1995.

Pitkin, Gary M., ed. *Cost-Effective Technical Services: How to Track, Manage, and Justify Internal Operations.* New York: Neal-Schuman, 1989. [Old, but good.]

Prentice, Ann E. *Financial Planning for Libraries.* 2nd ed. Lanham, MD: Scarecrow Press, 1996.

Rounds, Richard S., and Margo C. Trumpeter. *Basic Budgeting Practices for Libraries.* 2nd ed. Chicago: American Library Association, 1994.

Steele, Victoria, and Stephen D. Elder. *Becoming a Fundraiser: The Principles and Practice of Library Development.* Chicago: American Library Association, 2000.

Warner, Alice Sizer. *Budgeting: A How-to-Do-It Manual for Librarians.* New York: Neal-Schuman, 1998.

Wilder, Stanley J., et al. "Materials Budget Management: Good Practice, Good Politics." In *Technical Services Today and Tomorrow,* 2nd ed., edited by Michael Gorman, 53–65. Englewood, CO: Libraries Unlimited, 1998.

Note

1. Sometimes crossovers among the publications in cognate fields are helpful, e.g., the August 9, 2006, issue of *American Libraries Direct* quoted a report on school librarians' salaries for the previous year that had been published in *Education Week.* The study on which the report was based could be accessed through an online link, although the article on which it was based required a subscriber's password.

CHAPTER 7

Impact of Digital Resources

✧ Working with Metadata
✧ Building Local Digital Libraries
✧ Cooperative Collection-Development Projects
✧ Summary

TWENTY-FIRST-CENTURY library collections are a mix of traditional materials shelved in the library (books, maps, videos, music, pictures, drawings), which are, in most places, still the larger proportion of offerings, and digital resources delivered via computer wherever patrons have computers with appropriate connections, not solely in the library itself. Increasing numbers of libraries are acquiring digital resources as a significant and growing proportion of their collections. Because these resources are not merely a new type of object that gets purchased and placed on shelves in the usual way, their acquisition, organization, and maintenance are having a major impact on library organization and management.

Digital materials, known as electronic resources to catalogers, are not purchased but are leased by negotiating contracts with their owners or distributors. Libraries buy the right to access and use the materials but do not own them, and because the materials are electronic signals, when the right to access them ends, no physical objects are left in the library. Thus one of the main differences between traditional materials and new digital materials is that they are not ordered and paid for the same way. Contracts must be negotiated by people who understand the legal ramifications involved and can be signed only by those with the authority to do so. Such people may not even be part of the library's staff, let alone part of the technical services department.

Taking the following steps can improve the patron-catalog interface:

- Offer a whole range of library services to searchers, not solely indicate the presence or absence of a particular item in a library's collection.
- Employ graphics, sound, musical notation, and other indicators, as appropriate, to identify materials, especially visual images, maps, music and musical recordings, video recordings, and the like.
- Provide floor plans and maps in addition to call numbers.
- Give teasers, blurbs, reviews, and samples.
- Show covers, title pages, tables of contents, prefaces, and other preliminaries.
- Track previous searches and offer suggestions for similar materials.
- Show cross-reference retrieval sets without rekeying search statements.
- Provide a "Live Chat with a Librarian" button on every screen.

Source: Adapted from Sheila S. Intner, "Struggling toward Retrieval: Alternatives to Standard Operating Procedures Can Help Librarians and the Public," in *Electronic Cataloging: AACR2 and Metadata for Serials and Monographs* (New York: Haworth Information Press, 2003), 83.

Cataloging for digital materials also differs in important ways. First, the identifying information the cataloger creates is known as metadata. Second, unlike the records for traditional materials, which are always filed in a catalog physically separate from the materials, metadata can be an integral part of the materials themselves (embedded metadata). When not embedded, metadata provide links to the materials (associated metadata), obviating the need to locate materials as a separate operation. Finding the metadata *is* finding materials, not merely finding substitutes for the materials giving instructions about what the material is and where it is located. (Nevertheless, readers should be aware that links can break and, when they do, linked metadata are no different from ordinary catalog entries for traditional materials.)

This chapter discusses some of the challenges for technical services managers who are dealing with hybrid collections—part physical objects that libraries own outright, part digital signals that they contract to access for a limited time—including working with metadata, building local digital libraries, and participating in cooperative digital library projects.

Working with Metadata

Traditional library cataloging for digital resources is a kind of metadata creation. Imagine the following scenario: A library buys access to a database and when the contract is completed and approved, the buying office notifies the catalog department about the new acquisition so they can catalog it. A cataloger searches the library's bibliographic network for an existing record and uses this to create an entry for the library's catalog. If an existing record is not found, the cataloger creates a new record for the database following the rules of AACR2 and the library's chosen subject tools, codes the record into the MARC format, and both adds it to the library's catalog and uploads it to the bibliographic network. So far, digital materials follow the same procedures as books, videos, or other materials. What is the fuss over metadata all about?

The answer to the question is that library cataloging is not the only way to identify that new database for future retrieval. In some respects, it is the costliest and least efficient way to do the job. For one thing, although library catalogs are searchable on the World Wide Web, many searchers have trouble with the way they have to do it, entering exact subject headings taken from *Library of Congress Subject Headings* (LCSH) or requesting author names in authorized forms; for another thing, library cataloging does not take advantage of the capabilities of the same computers that transmit the databases to generate and transmit the metadata along with the resource. Other types of metadata respond to both these issues, offering easier ways to search and discover materials and being generated automatically from the databases, websites, images, or other electronic materials being transmitted. Metadata can also be created manually by metadata catalogers, a process that is easier than traditional cataloging. Once entered into the catalog system, metadata include links to the materials.

Working with systems for metadata creation other than traditional cataloging means learning what they are and how to construct and use them and applying selected metadata schemas to library materials.

One of the most frequently used metadata schemas is also one of the least complicated: Dublin Core. Dublin Core consists of fifteen data elements: Title, Subject, Description, Type, Source, Relation, Coverage, Creator, Publisher, Contributor, Rights, Date, Format, Identifier, and Language. Before entering a title, for example, the metadata cataloger enters an identifier showing that Dublin Core is being used, as in the following line:

<dc:title>Fundamentals of Technical Services Management</dc:title>

Librarians, especially catalogers, may see a resemblance to MARC in this type of data encoding. Unlike MARC, which also has protocols to identify data elements, Dublin Core does not specify how the data should be entered. A metadata cataloger can select any title to put into the title field, capitalizing or not, as desired. In contrast, MARC conforms to AACR2 and other library tools (LCSH, Dewey Decimal Classification, Library of Congress Classification, etc.), which have numerous rules governing how to select and enter data for every element. This makes MARC difficult for nonlibrarians to use. Dublin Core is easy to apply for librarians and nonlibrarians alike, but it allows for confusion when different metadata catalogers enter different titles (title page/screen title, cover title, spine title, menu title, caption, file name, etc.) for the same material or use multiple terms for the same subject.

Metadata librarians are often asked to do traditional cataloging for digital materials in addition to creating metadata. A new hire may be expected to make the most basic decisions about metadata standards and projects. Following are excerpts from job line and library press advertisements, seen in 2007:

> Supervises electronic and print cataloging processes . . . using the library's Innovative Interfaces ILS; ensures . . . compliance with national and local standards such as the MARC record. . . . Participates . . . in library digital projects, especially through the application of expertise in MeSH, UMLS and other appropriate vocabularies, as well as emerging national standards for metatagging bibliographic and other knowledge objects.

> Maintains expertise in metadata schemas and standards, and provides guidance within the division and the libraries in implementing them. Performs cataloging for monographs and integrating resources in all formats.

> While the primary focus of the work will be working with metadata for digital objects, this individual will also serve as the resident authority on traditional cataloging standards and emerging trends. . . . Select[s] the appropriate metadata scheme for digital projects.

Dublin Core is a general metadata element set, but it is not the only one used in the library community. More complex general schemas include MARCXML, which is a version of MARC format expressed in XML; MODS (Metadata Object Description Schema), which is a subset of MARC fields in XML format; and METS (Metadata Encoding and Transmission Standard), which includes protocols for encoding elements of information not covered by the other schemas (such as

S elected projects implementing the following metadata standards are documented:

DUBLIN CORE

- Colorado Digitization Project (Colorado State Library)
- Cooperative Online Resources Cataloging (OCLC)
- Foundations Project (State of Minnesota)
- Gateway to Educational Materials (U.S. Department of Education)
- Medical Metadata Project (Oregon Health Sciences University et al.)

METS

- Making of America (Library of Congress)
- FCLA Digital Archive (Florida Center for Library Automation)
- Ethnomusicological Video for Instruction and Analysis Digital Library (Indiana University and the University of Michigan)
- DSPACE (Massachusetts Institute of Technology)
- Peel's Prairie Provinces Project (University of Alberta)

MODS

- American Memory (Library of Congress)
- Bibutils (Ludwig Institute for Cancer Research)
- Chopin Early Editions (University of Chicago Library)
- DLF Aquifer Initiative (Digital Library Federation)
- TDL Repository (Texas Digital Library)

preservation information, for example). The added complexity of these schemas permits more detail in the encoding, which, in turn, increases the precision of the metadata.

Some subject-oriented and administratively linked communities have their own schemas. Examples of some of these communities and their schemas include the U.S. government, which designed Government Information Locator Service (GILS) for federal agencies to use; the education community, which uses Gateway to Educational Materials (GEM) and Learning Objects Metadata (LOM); and the art community, which designed Categories for the Description of Works of Art (CDWA) and Visual Resources Association Core (VRA Core). Ideally, searchers ought to be able to find the art-related materials they seek no matter what metadata schema is used to convey information about them, but the reality is that metadata schemas are not all interoperable and equally accessible to searchers.

What does all this mean for technical services department managers? It should mean two things: (1) that managers need

In response to an expressed need for metadata instruction in the library community at large, the Library of Congress, the Association for Library Collections and Technical Services, and the Program for Cooperative Cataloging have worked together to develop a curriculum that will introduce practicing librarians to metadata. Though still under development at this writing, selected courses have been tested in the field or offered as American Library Association preconferences in 2007. The curriculum includes the following:

1. Rules and Tools for Cataloging Internet Resources
2. Digital Project Planning and Management Basics
3. Metadata and Digital Library Development
4. Metadata Standards and Applications
5. Principles of Controlled Vocabulary and Thesaurus Design

to take on metadata creation (that is, the cataloging of library materials in digital form) as a new department function, and (2) that department staff need to gain the knowledge to work intelligently with metadata and digital materials. In some libraries, because metadata is similar to cataloging, directors assume technical services will take care of metadata needs, whether or not department staff members have the requisite knowledge. The manager's role in those instances is, first, to educate the director about the differences between traditional cataloging and metadata creation and, second, to obtain the required knowledge as well as to add staff, if they are needed.

In some libraries, because metadata creation involves digitized materials, directors assign it to their technology specialists (that is, the information technology [IT] department or computer department) without considering the impacts decisions about metadata might have on cataloging systems already in place under the technical services department's umbrella. The manager's role in those instances is to simultaneously forge links with the technologists' metadata staff and educate the director about the need for a close working relationship between the departments. Keeping abreast of what digital materials are being handled by the IT department and having input into the decisions being made about how those materials are organized in order to prevent barriers to interoperability are the immediate imperatives for the technical services department manager.

Building Local Digital Libraries

Building digital libraries is the newest activity being discussed in the library world for which outside funds (such as government grants) are available, and, as a result, local projects may seem to be attractive undertakings. Like all new activities, though, digital libraries present a variety of challenges, only some of which are obvious to the uninitiated. Practical, political, and financial issues must be addressed successfully, all of which takes time, energy, and creative thought as well as specialized knowledge. Most important of all is a clear understanding of who will use the resources contained in the digital library and how they will use them so that the right materials are included and the most appropriate organizational systems are selected to store and manage the materials and facilitate their use.

Any large undertaking involving computer networks and digitized materials tends to be costly, at least in the start-up stages, when all the components must be put in place for the first time. Moreover, new collections are costly to establish, and digital libraries are no exception.

Fundamental to success in starting any new collection, digital or otherwise, is a detailed picture of the need for the collection's contents (the products of the digital library project) and an equally detailed view of how to deliver the products to those who need them in a way that does not discourage use. In fact, building a digital library is a costly collection development project that deserves substantial commitment and careful planning.

Managers of technical services departments should be able to contribute at many points along the way in the planning and implementation of a local digital library project. At the same time, they should not be the sole decision makers, because such a project goes far beyond the metadata employed in its

Many elements are involved in ensuring that a digital library initiative succeeds. Among the features demonstrated by such successful projects as the Colorado Digitization Project (CDP), the California Digital Library (CDL), and JSTOR are the following:

1. Long-term commitment
2. Continuous development and expansion
3. Development of partnerships
4. Careful planning and consensus building
5. Securing the funding
6. Securing the personnel
7. Adoption of standards
8. Inclusiveness
9. Participant education

Source: Sheila S. Intner et al., *Metadata and Its Impact on Libraries* (Westport, CT: Libraries Unlimited, 2006), 185–87.

search-and-retrieval mechanism to understanding the public, the products, the delivery mechanisms, the equipment, and the overall relation of the project to the entire array of patron collections and services offered by the library. Technical services managers should be the leaders in establishing collection and organizational standards, facilitating and processing organizational and delivery mechanisms, and monitoring and evaluating such things as metadata effectiveness and collection use. Moreover, no technical services manager should accept the responsibility for metadata creation without concomitant authority to establish standards and maintain quality levels appropriate to the project.

Cooperative Collection-Development Projects

A growing number of large, successful, multilibrary digital library projects are under way and achieving important goals and objectives in the United States. Among these projects are the Library of Congress's American Memory program, the Colorado Digitization Project, the California Digital Library, the Cooperative Online Resource Catalog (CORC) initiated by OCLC, and Journal Storage (JSTOR).[1] Cooperation among a group of libraries has enabled these projects to accomplish several goals that are difficult for individual libraries to achieve, among them obtaining the needed funds, attracting and retaining knowledgeable staff, establishing and monitoring appropriate technologies and standards, continuously developing and expanding the collections, building partnerships that extend both the collection sources and potential markets, and sustaining a long-term commitment to the project.

In particular, the selection, establishment, and maintenance of metadata standards is a key to project success in multilibrary projects. When a local institution builds a digital library collection intended mainly for local use, the obligation to adopt standard systems and adhere to them strictly is less critical than when several institutions share their efforts and their materials. Sharing depends on interoperability, and interoperability depends on following a uniform set of standards or, in the absence of total agreement on a single standard, on following combinations of standards that do not raise insurmountable barriers to interoperability.

An advantage of multilibrary digital libraries is the likelihood that a greater number and variety of materials can be digitized, and more that are already in digital form can be added. Materials that have not been digitized before and are not duplicated in other databases are what make a digital library valuable to those who wish to use it, so a local institution's ability to extend its universe of potential materials beyond its own holdings is an important asset.

ARCHIVING AND PRESERVING DIGITAL MATERIALS

Why? Because electronic texts are subject to destruction inadvertently or due to the volatility of the medium, but their contents will be as important to scholars of the future as ancient texts are to contemporary scholars.

What? E-documents containing valuable intellectual or artistic contents that are readable, comprehensible, functional, and reflect the look and feel of the originals.

Who? E-document creators, publishers, distributors, systems administrators, libraries, archives, and users.

How? Refreshing the files, migrating files from one hardware/software configuration to another, and developing software that permits new hardware/software systems to read the original files.

How much? Costs of acquiring e-documents or of converting analog documents into digital form, plus the costs of maintaining the digital information over time.

Source: Adapted from Sheila S. Intner et al., *Metadata and Its Impact on Libraries* (Westport, CT: Libraries Unlimited, 2006), 195–219.

Summary

In principle, working with metadata is no different from working with other new collections, but in practice the implementation of serviceable systems is quite different. Similarly, the basics of gathering a digital collection resemble those for the gathering of any other new collection: to be useful, it must meet the needs of the people who will use it and be made available to them in an easy-to-use form. From the point of view of the technical services department, however, responsibility for acquiring digital materials can involve very different mechanisms and procedures from those used in acquiring traditional materials, mainly because of the volume of materials, the need to address matters of ownership and copyright, and the fact that the materials are not static and unchanging but evolve over time. In addition, working with the metadata schemas that organize the collection and make it possible for people to locate and obtain the materials they seek is different from providing traditional library cataloging.

Technical services departments may or may not be involved directly with digital library projects, although they are a logical locus for organizing activities, if not for managing the entire project. Department managers should work to educate directors and other decision makers about the need for interoperability among the cataloging systems used in managing both the traditional and the digital collections. Then, to the greatest degree possible, they should work with local colleagues and outside partners to select, establish, and maintain standard systems that facilitate a high degree of interoperability.

Recommended Reading

Building and Sustaining Digital Collections: Models for Libraries and Museums. Washington, DC: Council on Library and Information Resources, 2001.

Burgett, James, et al. *Collaborative Collection Development: A Practical Guide for Your Library.* Chicago: American Library Association, 2004.

Caplan, Priscilla. *Metadata Fundamentals for All Librarians.* Chicago: American Library Association, 2004.

Conger, Joan E. *Collaborative Electronic Resource Management: From Acquisitions to Assessment.* Westport, CT: Libraries Unlimited, 2004.

Hillman, Diane I., and Elaine L. Westbrooks, eds. *Metadata in Practice.* Chicago: American Library Association, 2004.

Intner, Sheila S., Susan S. Lazinger, and Jean Weihs. *Metadata and Its Impact on Libraries.* Westport, CT: Libraries Unlimited, 2006.

Jones, C. Wayne, et al., eds. *Cataloging the Web: Metadata, AACR, and MARC 21.* Lanham, MD: Scarecrow Press for the Association for Library Collections and Technical Services, 2002.

Smiraglia, Richard P., ed. *Metadata: A Cataloger's Primer.* New York: Haworth Information Press, 2005.

Note

1. These projects are described at their websites as follows:

   American Memory: http://memory.loc.gov/ammem/about/index .html (accessed December 27, 2006)

   Colorado Digitization Project: http://www.cdpheritage.org/reports Presentation.cfm (accessed December 27, 2006)

   California Digital Library: http://www.cdlib.org/glance/overview .html (accessed December 27, 2006)

   Cooperative Online Resource Catalog: http://www.oclc.org/ research/projects/archive/default.htm, p. 1 (accessed December 27, 2006)

   JSTOR: http://www.jstor.org/about/background.html (accessed December 27, 2006)

CHAPTER 8

Relationships beyond the Department

❖ Interacting with Others in the Library
❖ Interacting with the Library's Public
❖ Beyond the Library: Interacting with Peers and Outside Groups
❖ Summary

TECHNICAL SERVICES department managers generally represent the department in many kinds of official and unofficial interactions with people both within and outside of the library. They meet and discuss department activities with library administrators, heads of other library departments and their members, and members of the library's public. They meet with peers from other libraries and with interested businesspeople or professionals, often in pursuit of common goals such as building cooperative partnerships, buying products and services, and serving on committees of professional associations. They may speak to, counsel, and mentor students preparing for library careers. In all their interactions, technical services department managers have opportunities to highlight department contributions to information services. Good managers will take these interactions seriously and treat them with as much thought and care as they give to planning departmental work flow or writing annual reports.

Interacting with Others in the Library

The most frequent encounters a manager has beyond department borders are likely to be with others in the library: administrators, managers of other departments, librarians working in other departments, and members of the support staffs of other departments. The manager's demeanor is assumed to reflect the department's attitude toward the rest of the library staff. Depending on the way the manager treats them, others may perceive the department as open and collegial or closed and secretive, friendly and warm or haughty and distant, cooperative and ready to assist colleagues or cold to outsiders and indifferent to their problems.

Each manager has his or her own personal style, but those who tend toward either end of the personality continuum can benefit from a dose of behavior modification. Whether one is, by nature, overly shy, introspective, and cold or overly assertive, enthusiastic, and extroverted, extreme behaviors raise doubts about one's abilities, motives, and agenda. Good managers should aim for a balanced style of interaction that emphasizes courtesy and respect for others and gives evidence that their department shares in the work of the library and tries to be helpful for the good of the entire group.

Some managers find it difficult to advocate for their department without engaging in behavior that makes them appear callous to the needs of other departments. Library directors contribute to this posture when they play a zero-sum game in which one department is pitted against another to compete for limited funds. These directors may think that competition keeps managers on their toes and encourages productivity. In fact, that kind of atmosphere can be poisonous, making managers defensive, secretive, selfish, and too quick to restrict their activities solely to those they believe curry favor, regardless of the impact on the library and patron services as a whole.

Good managers should act positively and assertively on behalf of their departments but do so in a way that does not simultaneously hurt other departments or affect service negatively. When money is short and budget requests must be defended vigorously, good managers should demonstrate how money spent in their department meets the library's overall goals and objectives. They should never argue that other departments have an unfair share of the resources or that others perform poorly, waste money, or fail to meet their responsibilities. Describing the good performance of their department and the results they can produce is the managers' job. Pointing out the bad performance of others is not.

Working smoothly with others on library-wide initiatives is another important way technical services managers help establish a good reputation for their department. Similarly, encouraging and facilitating participation of department staff members on library committees and projects adds positively to departmental visibility and image.

Interacting with Library Administrators

One of the most important responsibilities of a department manager is working with superiors on several levels: presenting department plans, budgets, and requests; answering questions about department activities and capabilities; responding promptly to administrative requests; and reporting regularly and accurately about department activities. Good managers must strike a balance between being cooperative and flexible when that kind of approach is called for and standing firm and supporting department needs when those needs are key to getting the work done. Part of the skill of serving as a middle manager, which is what department heads are, is being able to negotiate the fine line between departmental allegiance and subservience to superiors. Both the upper-level administrators to whom managers report and the departmental staff whom managers supervise should be able to trust (and rightfully so) that managers consider *their* needs and are fair *to them* in making decisions and setting priorities.

Similarly, department managers need to educate their superiors about department goals and objectives, production, problems and potential solutions, staff members, sources, products, and so on. No one else in the library has more knowledge or better purpose in helping

If it has not already done so, e-mail will soon supersede face-to-face meetings, memoranda, and telephone conversations as the most popular method of communicating information among the managers and staff of technical services departments as well as with managers and staff of other departments, administrators, suppliers, patrons, and others. David Angell and Brent Heslop suggest ways to ensure e-mails are courteous:

- Don't flame.
- Respect confidentiality.
- Watch what you say.
- Protect yourself against hackers.
- Be careful about copyrights and licenses.
- Eliminate sexist language.
- Be culturally aware.
- Avoid using all capital letters (also known as "shouting").
- Avoid using all lowercase letters.
- Check your e-mail regularly.
- Know when not to use e-mail.

Source: David Angell and Brent Heslop, *The Elements of E-mail Style: Communicate Effectively via Electronic Mail* (Reading, MA: Addison-Wesley, 1994), 4–13.

superiors understand the department's role in the library and, more important, the department's contribution to library-wide goals and objectives. Interactions with superiors are opportunities to describe, explain, and supply information about the department, provided that the manager does so skillfully, as a natural part of an exchange.

Interacting with Other Department Managers

The technical services department's activities affect other departments directly or indirectly, and a wise manager will work to develop and maintain good relations with peers from other departments. Acquisitionists within technical services directly affect collection-building outcomes; catalogers affect the quality and effectiveness of the public catalog, the library's main information tool; preservationists' and processors' efforts can have dramatic impacts on collection performance. It is hard to imagine any direct public service that does not depend to some extent on activities of the technical services department, and responsibility for the results, whether good or bad, is attributed to the department manager.

Good relations take work, time, thought, and perseverance. Relationships develop slowly over time and require sustained effort. It might seem difficult to work opportunities for continuing contact with peers into a busy schedule, but informal sharing can count, too, because formal meetings are devoted to business. Lunches, coffee breaks, and volunteer activities create opportunities for informal sharing with peers. So does offering or agreeing to share a common commute or a leisure-time activity. A manager can seek ways in which the pursuit of similar interests and obligations will provide extra time to get to know peers better. Learning what is important to others can be helpful when mutual problems need to be solved. Choosing the most agreeable alternative based on such knowledge can shorten a lengthy negotiation process.

Interacting with Librarians and Staff from Other Departments

New technical services managers may be surprised to discover that librarians and staff working in other departments know very little or have incorrect ideas about what goes on in technical services. This could be due to a few grains of truth in the stereotype of technical services staff, namely that they speak only to one another because no one else understands their jargon or because they are too introverted to talk to outsiders. Good managers should designate themselves first on a list that includes the whole department staff to take responsibility for dispelling the stereotype. Dispelling the stereotype means speaking in terms that listeners can understand, being ready and willing to hear other viewpoints, listening to what others have to say, and finding topics of common interest.

Some helpful points to keep in mind when talking with people who work outside the department are the following:

Do not assume your listeners are familiar with the issues, problems, people, or organizations with which you deal on a regular basis. Instead, ask if they are and explain as necessary, not only so you are understood but also to inform your listeners about things they might find useful to know.

Be interested in hearing about the issues, problems, people, and organizations with which your listeners deal on a regular basis. Ask questions, listen to explanations, and take the opportunity to learn about them.

Look for common ground and mutual interests as well as ways in which the methods and solutions of others might be applied productively to technical services. If it is helpful, describe how you solved a problem similar to one your listener has.

Be businesslike about business, keeping to the subject and doing the work before indulging in social conversation. However, at the same time, be aware that some people feel obliged to indulge in a few minutes of social conversation before tackling business, so be sensitive to that possibility and respond appropriately.

Put yourself in your listeners' shoes when discussing mutual problems and always aim for win-win solutions that have no negative impact on their work. At the same time, explain gently but firmly if your listeners' proposed solutions affect your work negatively. Do not give up until you reach a solution in which nobody loses.

Interacting with the Library's Public

In large libraries, technical services librarians, including managers, are unlikely to have many official interactions with members of the

Honing your communication skills can do more than make you a better trainer and communicator within your department. It can lead to invitations to speak in public or write for publication, especially if you are also an active volunteer in professional associations and service organizations. Such opportunities are to be welcomed because they have important advantages, despite the fact that they involve hard work, most often done on your own time. Among the advantages to be gained from public speaking, writing, and publishing are the following:

1. You can disseminate new ideas and suggestions for solving common problems and share the results of your experiences.
2. You gain access to appropriate outlets for results of research and experimentation.
3. You can contribute to better management of technical services in peer libraries.
4 You gain stature for your library and your department as well as for yourself.

public. In small and medium-sized libraries, however, technical services personnel may be scheduled to staff the information desk for some part of their workweek, answering questions and giving direct service to patrons. Those interactions can be challenging because there is no way of knowing what questions will be asked, but they are also enjoyable and satisfying when answers are found and patrons appreciate the assistance. Managers can be supportive of assignments to the information desk (both their own, if they take their turns at the desk, and those of their staff members), or they can be resentful of the time it takes away from department activities. Such resentment can carry over to staff, making them, too, resentful and, in the long run, less effective.

Since desk assignments probably cannot be avoided, it behooves good managers to accept them graciously and think about how they

5. You increase your visibility and improve your likelihood of receiving more invitations at higher levels that provide opportunities for interesting travel, meeting new colleagues, and learning from new experiences.

6. As your reputation builds, you may be offered formal consulting jobs that directly affect others' efficiency, productivity, and product quality and enable their libraries to save money. You also earn added income.

7. You may be encouraged to earn new credentials, such as a Ph.D., adding both to your own knowledge and to our field's body of professional knowledge.

Bear in mind that as Walt Crawford eloquently expounds in his book about writing and speaking,* first you must have something to say that is worth the reader's or listener's time.

---

* Walt Crawford, *First Have Something to Say: Writing for the Library Profession* (Chicago: American Library Association, 2003).

could benefit the department. For example, interacting with the public enables catalogers to hear firsthand what causes trouble when patrons search the catalog and what helps them succeed. Acquisitionists and serialists can learn what titles are most needed and why, which may make them more sensitive to expediting orders for materials patrons need before specific deadlines. Preservationists can get a better idea of titles likely to receive heavy use and take the opportunity when speaking with patrons requesting such material to explain good handling techniques.

The old adage "If you can't beat 'em, join 'em" is true when it comes to technical services staff members working at the desk. The last thing good managers should want is to have department members labeled incompetent or unpleasant when working with the public. Being bad at a job might get someone out of it, but a bad reputation follows the person and taints whatever else he or she does. Instead, persuade staff members to make the most of the assignments by encouraging them to establish relationships with patrons and report what they learn back to the department. The knowledge obtained through desk work can inform decisions made within the technical services department about setting priorities and fine-tuning procedures.

Managers can also make a case for two-way cooperation, that is, having information desk staff take turns working in the technical services department. Are special language skills needed? Knowledge of special materials? Historical information? Often, members of the information desk staff have such skills and could be requested for specific or ongoing tasks within technical services. The dual department assignments can create welcome changes of pace and venue for people who would otherwise have relatively limited variation in their work.

Beyond the Library: Interacting with Peers and Outside Groups

Technical services department managers typically interact with their counterparts from other libraries in professional associations, user groups, and other organizations outside the library. They may be chosen to serve on vendors' advisory councils, multilibrary cooperative organization committees, state or regional boards and steering committees, and the like. Serving well in these capacities and gaining a reputation for being an active participant who is competent, dependable, trustworthy, and creative can go far in advancing not only a manager's own career but also the reputation of the technical services department.

The same qualities that make someone a good manager—displaying strong communication and listening skills; being courteous, respectful, and fair to others; knowing how to analyze problems and find solutions; working hard and willingly taking on a fair share of the burdens of any job; and dealing comfortably with people at all levels—make it likely that person interacts effectively with his or her peers and other people representing outside groups. Likewise, the same things that make people hard to work with—failure to communicate, saying one thing and doing another, unnecessarily keeping helpful information secret, avoiding responsibility, blaming others for problems, and taking credit for the work of others—also tend to carry over to interactions with peers and outside groups.

Summary

This chapter examined technical services department managers' interactions with people within and outside of their libraries, including the heads of other departments, staff members working in other departments, senior administrators, patrons, peers (that is, technical services department managers working in other libraries), and representatives of outside organizations.

Tips for successful interactions:

- Accentuate the positive aspects of every interaction, whether it is part of your job or a wholly voluntary activity.
- Know why you are participating, what you can contribute, and what benefits you hope to achieve.
- Participate willingly but be clear about your limits in terms of time and contribution because, in the long run, overcommitment rarely does anyone any good.
- Behave toward others the same way you want others to behave toward you.

Functioning as a strong advocate for one's department does not have to mean competing with other departments unfairly or in a strident and offensive manner. Basing arguments on one's own department's strengths and avoiding the temptation to talk about other departments' weaknesses can go far in retaining respect and collegiality with other department managers.

In the long run, the best advice for any manager is "be yourself." Far from being a platitude, this seemingly simple piece of advice has a far-from-simple meaning. A consistent demeanor that emphasizes courtesy, reflects professionalism, and expresses a positive, principled approach to matters of mutual concern is the best policy, not only because it is likely to be the most satisfying personally but also because it tends to elicit good responses from others.

CHAPTER 9

Evaluating the Department

by Peggy Johnson

✧ What Is Evaluation and Why Do It?
✧ Evaluating Operations in the Technical Services Unit
✧ Criteria for Effective Evaluation
✧ Measures and Standards
✧ Evaluation Equals Action
✧ Summary

FOR MANY LIBRARIES, evaluation has focused on collecting statistics—counting something, such as dollars in a budget, volumes added, titles cataloged, items in an uncataloged backlog, or perhaps length of time between an item's receipt and its availability on the shelf. Libraries have a history of successfully counting things (inputs and outputs) and some success in measuring the effectiveness of specific projects in reaching stated objectives. Increasingly, attention has been given to evaluating library services and areas that have direct bearing on users, such as reference and information services, instruction, collections, web pages, shelf availability, and document delivery. Evaluating performance in technical services can be more challenging than in other library units because it is difficult to draw direct correlations between work done and its impact on users. Nevertheless, performance evaluation is a critical component in effectively managing a technical services unit.

What Is Evaluation and Why Do It?

Evaluation is an analytical tool for identifying effectiveness and failures and improving services. Evaluation depends on data, which provide the facts on which decisions are based. It is applied both to specific projects (Is the project on track to meet stated goals? Did it accomplish what it set out to do?) and the ongoing operations of a unit (Are backlogs being avoided? Have allocated funds been spent? Were annual performance targets met?). Ideally, evaluation links directly to the library's mission and to the goals and objectives of the library and the unit being evaluated. Evaluation is part of the planning cycle. Without clear goals and objectives against which to measure progress and accomplishments, evaluation is impossible. Without data, decisions are made on assumptions, not based on facts.

Evidenced-based librarianship is a new term being used in discussions of library evaluation. It is derived from evidence-based medicine, an approach to medical care in which physicians use the current best evidence to make decisions about the care of patients. Booth defined evidence-based librarianship as "an approach to information science that promotes the collection, interpretation, and integration of valid, important, and applicable user-reported, librarian-observed, and research-derived evidence. The best available evidence, moderated by user needs and preferences, is applied to improve the quality of professional judgments."[1] This concept emphasizes the need to be rigorous in data collection and analysis and to use what is learned to make the best possible decisions.

Lancaster suggests looking at evaluation in terms of costs, effectiveness, and benefits.[2] Costs are the dollars expended in paying staff salaries; purchasing services from vendors, utilities, and agents; supporting training; and so forth. Effectiveness is measured in terms of how well a service or operation satisfies the demand placed upon it by its stakeholders or users or both. Are materials rush cataloged quickly enough to satisfy user requests for them? Did a unit overspend its allocated budget? Benefits are the positive results of an action or activity. Can users find the resources they need through the catalog?

Effectiveness pertains to whether the right tasks are being performed in the correct manner. Cost-effectiveness reflects internal operating efficiency. Efficiency relates to the number of items processed or tasks accomplished in a specified amount of time. In a cost-effective unit, the allocation and expenditure of resources are managed to achieve the highest quality of services possible given the funds allowed. Striking a reasonable balance between cost and effectiveness requires judgment. A classic challenge related to cost-effective cataloging is deciding how much should be invested (in local salary dollars or, perhaps, in purchasing vendor records) to obtain the very best catalog records balanced against the benefit of providing records that are good enough to help most users. A cost-effective unit focuses on performing tasks and operations well and pursues higher quality only if additional funds are available and their investment will yield worthwhile benefits.

Cost-benefit analysis examines whether the value of a service is more or less than the cost of providing it. It looks at economic feasibility and economic viability. The problem with cost-benefit analysis that confronts libraries is how to demonstrate benefit or value. How much is a library user's time worth? How can the cost of adding tables of contents to catalog records be measured in benefits to the catalog user? Cost-benefit analysis evaluates both monetary and nonmonetary costs and benefits. It differs from cost-effectiveness studies, which seek to maximize performance output in relation to input costs, and cost-efficiency studies, which aim to minimize input costs while maintaining efficiency. Hernon and McClure point out that a critical point exists between efficiency and effectiveness at which "increasing the performance of either the effectiveness or efficiency of a service diminishes the performance of the other."[3] Identifying and operating at this critical point is facilitated by effective evaluation. Good service and efficiency and effectiveness are not mutually exclusive. Evaluation—when done well—assists managers in making better decisions, identifying aspects of operations that might be improved, and targeting processes and activities that can be made more effective, more efficient, or less expensive.

Lancaster and McCutcheon distinguish between macroevaluation and microevaluation.[4] Macroevaluation examines the level of performance of a service or system. It tells how a unit is performing and usually measures against standards or benchmarks. As such, macroevaluation can provide a local baseline against which changes in the system can be measured over time. Microevaluation is interpretative and informs decisions about what needs to be done to raise the level of performance. It identifies sources of failure (e.g., poorly trained staff, undependable technology, or insufficient staffing levels) and inefficiencies (e.g., poorly designed work flow or failure to use appropriate technological tools) with the aim of addressing them. Microevaluation gathers the information necessary to identify problems and to fix them. It requires analysis of findings and leads to improvement.

Libraries evaluate their operations and services for many purposes. Simple counting and measuring of inputs and outputs may be done because such data are required for an annual report to local administration, as part of external reporting obligations, or as the final report for a grant-funded project. Evaluation can help identify activities or processes that need additional study. It can serve as an internal control mechanism and a way to demonstrate accountability—that is, effective stewardship of resources. Such reports can justify continued funding or increased allocations and provide guidance in allocating funds among programs. Data collected can be used to support grant proposals. Evaluation can aid in making decisions about a program, service, or function—whether it should be adjusted or refocused in some way or whether it should be continued or discontinued.

Another important reason for evaluating is to facilitate communication. Evaluations document outcomes to stakeholders—others within the library, users, funding agencies, and governing boards. It can serve as a means for promoting accomplishments as well as for documenting needs. It can provide immediate feedback to work groups and to

E ffective performance measures should be related to goals, be meaningful and easily understood, and be used effectively and deliberately. If a library has a goal to move materials to the stacks more quickly, it may begin by collecting baseline data on time between item receipt and completion of cataloging and marking. After setting a throughput goal (e.g., 80 percent of items to be completed within two weeks), it will review and revise the various steps involved. Once the process improvements are implemented, data are collected and measured against the baseline data and the target. The figure below indicates that initially 75 percent of materials took twenty-one days or more to move through the unit; after goals were set and changes implemented, 50 percent of materials moved through in fourteen days or fewer.

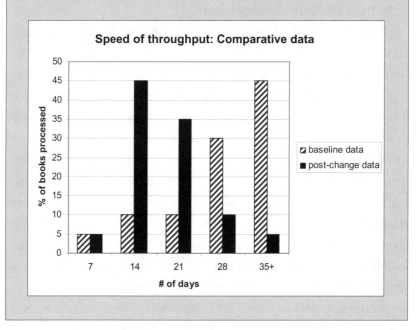

individuals on how well they are performing. As part of the planning process, evaluation can provide a framework for staff to use in assessing their progress toward goals and suggesting course corrections if problems are identified.

Childres and Van House have identified four interrelated questions that are answered by effective evaluation:

- To what extent doe the organization achieve its goals?
- To what extent is the organization a healthy operating unit?
- To what extent can the organization capture from the external environment the resources needed to survive or thrive?
- To what extent are the various stakeholders' priorities met?[5]

To answer these questions, performance measures and performance goals should be meaningful, easily understood, and effectively and deliberately used.

Evaluating Operations in the Technical Services Unit

In most technical services units, performance and activities are measured by counting inputs (e.g., orders received from selectors, titles received from suppliers) and outputs (e.g., orders placed, titles cataloged, authority records created). This macroevaluation is valuable for comparing performance month to month and year to year and against explicit goals. These statistics may be collected either through manual tally sheets or computer-system-generated reports or both. Not everything can be counted using automated methods. For example, the number of boxes of books received daily from vendors, the number of vendor errors in a shipment, or the number and type of individual catalog record errors reported to the technical services unit need to be counted manually. Another form of manual data collection uses survey sheets on which staff members report the amount of time devoted to specified tasks, for example, the length of time required to catalog different types of materials or to create different cataloging records (original or copy). For example, a study at the Carnegie Mellon University

In a discussion about evaluating the catalogers she supervised at the University of California, Irvine, D. Kathryn Weintraub suggested using database management software to track performance and isolate areas in which particular catalogers needed training. In a follow-up, Weintraub described the positive impact of using spreadsheets to monitor quality of output and emphasized that managers need to be sensitive to the following matters:

Respect the privacy of the data; do not share spreadsheets with anyone but the cataloger whose work they report and do not use them for personnel evaluation unless the cataloger is aware they will be used this way before tracking begins.

Know that experienced professionals do not use data to compete against one another; individuals compete solely with their own performance.

Expect that, generally, data will reveal improvements in the quality of output over time.

Expect data to reveal gaps in knowledge specific to individuals; once identified, knowledge gaps can be remedied with added training.

Use data as hard evidence of the increasing quality of department products.

Sources: D. Kathryn Weintraub, "Using Management Tools for Cataloging Discussions," in *Recruiting, Educating, and Training Cataloging Librarians: Solving the Problems,* ed. Sheila S. Intner and Janet Swan Hill (Westport, CT: Greenwood Press, 1989), 375–89; D. Kathryn Weintraub, "On the Job Training: Issues and Answers," in *Cataloging, the Professional Development Cycle,* ed. Sheila S. Intner and Janet Swan Hill (Westport, CT: Greenwood Press, 1991), 119–23.

Libraries used survey sheets and determined that 83 percent of monographs were cataloged in less than fifteen minutes.[6]

Work-flow analysis is another manual approach for gathering data for evaluation. Work-flow mapping, sometimes called flowcharting, tracks the sequence of tasks and decision points in a process. A similar technique is work-path charting, which maps the physical movement of materials through a unit. Both approaches can help identify inefficiencies and problems that result from the way tasks are organized, decisions are made, staff are deployed, and work is scheduled. They may also reveal wasted or duplicated effort (perhaps unnecessary hand-offs of work).

Libraries that use automated library systems usually can obtain several types of quantitative statistics, including orders placed, titles cataloged, volumes added, and so on, from the system itself. Some systems can generate custom on-demand reports or permit writing programs to create a greater variety of reports. These reports might, for example, use the dates on which operations were performed within the automated system and generate reports showing the average time that elapses between actions. One example would be a report that calculates the average length of time between receipting an item and creating a catalog record.

One possible approach to gathering data on user perceptions of the department's operations is use of focus groups consisting of library employees from units outside of technical services. Elhard and Jin reported on a project that used such focus groups to assess cataloging services.[7] In a research project at the University of Illinois, the authors focused on communication issues and sought qualitative data to integrate with more traditional quantitative data. Through their research, they identified problem areas and took steps to address them.

The collection of data is a part of evaluation but not the goal. Analyzing data moves evaluation from the macro level to the micro level. Efficiency is usually a key goal in technical services. Time and cost studies are a common approach to evaluating the efficiency of technical services operations. Time and cost studies do not reveal whether backlogs exist or are being created; they measure only current work flow. Time can be the length of time necessary to perform an operation (e.g., place an order or mark a book) or the time elapsed (e.g., length of time between cataloging an item and marking it for the shelf or between receipt of a request to order placement). Costs are dollar values assigned to tasks, functions, or services. If a library calculates the average cost of locally cataloging a book plus the cost of marking it, the library can compare this total to the cost of purchasing catalog records and having books delivered shelf-ready from a vendor. Hewett notes that cost studies aid in "making certain types of decisions more objective, or at least demonstrably conscious."[8] The Carnegie cataloging time study went beyond simply measuring the average time required to catalog an item to identifying and analyzing the problems that catalogers encountered and that lengthened the time spent on a single item.[9]

Technical services managers have long sought generally accepted time and cost estimates (benchmarks) for functions that occur in most technical services units. Benchmarks allow comparison of local performance against other libraries, ideally against those that are exhibiting high levels of performance. External benchmarks from high-performing libraries indicate best practices, which might then be adopted locally. This is sometimes called competitive benchmarking in the corporate sector. If external benchmarks for performance were available, libraries could more easily determine how locally performed operations compare to these norms, if adjustments would improve performance, and if outsourcing operations would be less costly than handling them internally. Unfortunately, such generally accepted benchmarks do not exist. A study by McCain and Shorten sought to address this deficiency by surveying twenty-six academic libraries, identifying six that exhibited best practices, and comparing outputs for these libraries in five areas: volumes cataloged per full-time equivalent (FTE), titles cataloged per FTE, authority updates per FTE, holdings updates per FTE, and original cataloging per FTE.[10] Their findings reveal astounding ranges in all five areas. For example, volumes cataloged annually varied from 867 to 5,028 per FTE in the libraries identified as having best practices. Even data from the most effective libraries do not provide generally applicable performance standards.

Many technical services units have conducted time and cost studies; however, the results are presented as illustrations of process, not as standards or goals for other libraries. Most notable are the several studies conducted at Iowa State University.[11] Hurlbert and Dujmic make no claims that their evaluation at Carnegie provides data that are applicable elsewhere or could be used for performance standards at other libraries.[12]

Benchmarking is an organized process for measuring products, services, and practices against external partners to achieved performance. . . . After learning how well a library does it now, one learns from others how they do it and then applies what has been learned to make the library's operations or service better. The process of benchmarking is often associated with the phrase 'best practices.'"

Source: Joseph R. Matthews, *The Bottom Line: Determining and Communicating the Value of the Special Library* (Westport, CT: Libraries Unlimited, 2002), 49.

Local costs vary because of differences in levels of staff doing comparable tasks, salaries for similar classifications of staff, work flow, and overhead costs. For the most part, each library must establish its own benchmarks for performance and baseline data for time and costs in order to perform internal analyses and comparisons and to compare against possible external alternatives.

Criteria for Effective Evaluation

Effective evaluation has several characteristics: it relates to stated local goals, and it is library-specific and individualized to the local situation and environment. The purposes of the evaluation should be clear. What questions need to be answered? What information is required to answer these questions? What data will be collected and from where? Who needs the data? How does this specific set of data relate to other data being collected? How will the data be collected and who will do the collection? When will the data be collected and how frequently? Who will manipulate, analyze, and interpret the data? Who will present the results to others? How will this reporting be done and how frequently? Who will act on it?

The data collected should be useful, and their collection should have a clear purpose. Data are documented facts, information, or evidence. They should have meaning in the local context in order to inform decision making. Some libraries use the phrase *metrics that matter* to describe the measures on which they focus. Measures used in evaluation are both quantitative and qualitative. Quantitative measures focus on quantities or amounts of items, whereas qualitative measures are descriptive and do not involve numbers or measures. The American Society for Quality notes that *quality* can have two meanings: "the characteristics of a product or service that bear on its ability to satisfy stated or implied needs" and "a product or service free of deficiencies."[13] Quality is subjective and, like beauty, in the eye of the beholder.

Counting orders placed or titles cataloged is straightforward. Measuring the quality of an order record is more subjective. Is it good enough for a vendor to know which item to supply? Is it good enough to prevent duplicate orders from being placed? A good-quality order record might be defined as one that saves time in cataloging once the item arrives. Measuring the quality of cataloging is a perennial problem in technical services units. The Library of Congress held a symposium on this topic in 1995 and concluded that quality cataloging is "accurate bibliographic information that meets the users' needs and provides appropriate access in a timely fashion."[14] This statement prompts a question that has yet to be answered: What are users' needs? The relative values of accuracy and fullness in catalog records and speed in their creation need further study. An individual library must define its own standards for quality and quantity.

To be meaningful, the data collected should satisfy several conditions. They should be reliable. Reliability is the consistency of a measurement or the degree to which an instrument measures the same way each time it is used under the same conditions with the same subjects. In short, the findings are repeatable. In addition, the data should be valid, that is, appropriate to the formulation of relevant and meaningful conclusions, inferences, or propositions. The results should be repeatable, comparable, and cumulative. The data should be collected in a manner that supports comparison over time. Monthly and annual productivity counts generally are comparative. The data collected should be accurate and precise, within reason. In other words, a margin of error is acceptable and does not nullify the findings. Libraries that use manual tally sheets to track serial-issue check-in realize that the clerk may miss making a few hash marks in the course of a month, and they consider these modest discrepancies tolerable. The cost and effort of gathering the data should be acceptable.

Simple methods of collecting data are often the least costly. Data might be gathered through representative sampling and at predetermined times during a year in order to keep costs manageable. If sampling is used, consideration should be given to the sample size, sampling period, data-collection intervals, and how the sample is selected (random, etc.). Sampling periods should be chosen carefully so that results are not skewed by the time of year, staff absences, and so on. If sampling is done once a year, the same time should be used when repeating the data collection in subsequent years.

Working with numerical data requires careful attention. While spreadsheet software is an essential tool for organizing and manipulating data, it does not negate the needs for mathematical skills and common sense. If formulas are used, they should be clear, logical, and mathematical. Rounding up or down should not have an adverse effect on numbers. If an average is calculated, important data should not be lost. In some cases, an average has little meaning. For example, a technical services unit may report that the average time required to mark a book is twenty-four hours. If, however, 75 percent of the books are marked in eight hours or less, then 25 percent of the books are lingering for much longer in the marking room. Thoughtful analysis of the data will indicate a problem that needs attention. Numbers must be entered accurately, and formulas should be reviewed. Unexpected changes should be investigated. One library system counted the number of user visits by recording daily counts from security-system one-way entrances in all locations. One of the branch libraries got a new gate system that recorded each body that went through it, whether entering or exiting. A staff member entered a formula ($N \div 2$) in the spreadsheet to calculate the actual number of visits. Unfortunately, she entered the formula in a cell that referred to another location, resulting in one library's use appearing to drop by 50 percent and another's appearing to double. Simply recording numbers is never sufficient. Everyone involved in data gathering should understand why the data are being collected and be attentive to their accuracy, meaning, and implications.

No measures of performance are right or wrong. The challenges are selecting those that are correct for the specific technical services unit and meet local needs (for reporting out, for analysis, etc.), designing them well, and applying them carefully and consistently. Libraries have a tendency to collect data that are not needed or that are not meaningful. They often fail to pay sufficient attention to why the data are collected or what is done with them. Data should be collected and analyzed in order to make better decisions. Measures are not an end in themselves and should not be seen simply as something to be reported. They offer a resource for improving operations and services, provided the appropriate measures are used.

Measures and Standards

Measures gauge specific data and typically are expressed in terms of quantity, time, quality, or cost. That is, measures can be counts of items (serial issues receipted), amounts of time (time lapse between order placement and item receipt), degrees of quality (acceptable error rate), or units of money (dollars encumbered per month). Stueart and Moran define *standards* as "any measure by which one judges a thing as authentic, good, or adequate. They should provide guidance for actions in the present climate while being flexible enough to allow for future developments."[15] Standards are the established and accepted norms against which subsequent activities or outcomes are compared in order to assess those activities or outcomes. Standards in libraries are performance guidelines rather than requirements or mandated specifications that must be met. Standards, while generally desired by managers, can make technical services staff uncomfortable because they can be perceived as mandatory. Bénaud, Bordeianu, and Hanson observed that "words such as *quotas, norms, output,* or *throughput* . . . are emotionally charged for some catalogers."[16] This is also often true for staff members in other technical services units—acquisitions staff, serials staff, marking staff, and so on.

While standards do have a role in personnel evaluation, they serve a critical function in the assessment of overall technical services operations because they permit the comparison of a project's outcome or a unit's performance against an accepted norm or a goal. For example, a library might receive a National Endowment for the Humanities preservation and access grant to conserve and catalog 8,000 nineteenth-century children's books. During the two years of the grant, the technical services unit's responsibility is to catalog the books. To process all 8,000 books, the cataloging unit must average 333 titles per month (realizing that counts may be lower in the first few months and increase thereafter). Regardless of how the work is distributed and the type of cataloging required, the standard of performance for the unit is clear.

Ongoing work in a unit can be measured against standards as well. While standards for numbers of units (orders, titles, issues, etc.) are more rare, many libraries set standards for throughput, for example, that monographic orders will be placed within forty-eight hours of receipt, that serial issues will be checked in within twenty-four hours of receipt, or that copy cataloging will be completed within two weeks of item receipt. A unit's success in performing at these standards can be measured through periodic data collection.

Annual performance standards (sometimes described as targets), like project performance standards, usually have milestones against which progress is gauged. Units normally have an annually allocated salary budget. One measure of performance is often equitable spending of the funds over the course of the fiscal year. A unit that has expended 75 percent of its salary budget in the first four months will likely have difficulty. Conversely, failure to expend a budget suggests a different kind of problem. Another approach might be as simple as using the total number of monographs acquired annually as part of the standard against which the number of titles cataloged annually is measured. In both examples, standards serve to assess the extent to which targets are met or goals accomplished. Standards serve as performance indicators and are a means of measuring achievement.

One advantage of clearly understood standards is a shared sense of responsibility for performance and a personal as well as a shared sense of accountability. Standards and performance measures can facilitate effective and efficient performance. They do run the risk of inducing dysfunctional behaviors if the measures do not provide a complete and balanced picture of desired outcomes. This returns to the equilibrium that each technical services unit must define for itself based on local goals for inputs, outputs, outcomes, effectiveness, efficiency, quality, and quantity.

Some libraries are applying concepts developed in the business world to select key performance measures. One approach adopted by a few libraries is a technique known as the balanced scorecard.[17] The idea behind this technique is to allow the library (or unit) to concentrate on a small number of measures that, when taken together, provide a quick and comprehensive picture of its operational well-being. Performance indicators across equally significant perspectives or areas are combined to produce a balanced evaluation. In the traditional approach to developing a balanced scorecard, measures are created for financial issues, users (internal, external, or both), internal processes, and improvement activities. The goal is to avoid achieving improvements in one area at the expense of another. These measures are sometimes called key measures or dashboard measures. While data likely will continue to be collected in many areas, key or critical measures are selected as generally indicative of success.

Physicians use a key measures approach when they check a patient's body temperature, blood pressure, pulse, and weight and compare newly gathered data to data from the patient's last visit. The data serve as medical key measures, and noteworthy deviations from one set of data to the next will result in further investigation to identify problems and explore solutions. Physicians use a form of benchmarking as well when they compare the results of an individual's laboratory tests, such as cholesterol levels, to norms for healthy people.

Patient Name	Examination Date	Examination Date
Temperature		
Blood pressure		
Pulse		
Weight		
Height		

A technical services unit might select the following dashboard measures:

- Cumulative percentage of acquisitions budget encumbered by month
- Average time lapsed between selection and order placement
- Number of orders placed
- Average time elapsed between item receipt and item availability
- Percentage of materials received shelf-ready with cataloging copy
- Number of titles receiving original cataloging

- Number of items cataloged from backlog or other uncataloged collections
- Number of cataloging errors reported/corrected

These data represent only a small portion of the activities that occur in a technical services unit, yet variations from the goals, targets, or performance standards likely would indicate problems in other areas and guide intervention and correction at several points. Dashboard measures can be posted on a technical services unit website or perhaps on a poster in the unit, where staff members can easily see and monitor activities. Figure 9.1 offers one example of a key measure in a library that is aiming to increase the number of items arriving shelf-ready to 45 percent of new receipts. It compares numbers of shelf-ready materials received over the course of one year during which additional services were purchased from vendors. Another simple approach might be to post a thermometer-like chart showing a goal (perhaps eliminating the backlog) at the top with gradients darkened in for each increment accomplished. Each change highlights a key measure of progress and is easy for staff members and stakeholders to grasp.

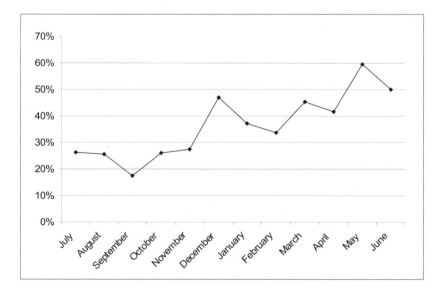

Figure 9.1   Percentage of total orders received shelf-ready

Evaluation Equals Action

Evaluation should not happen just once or even just once a year. It is not an end in itself. It is a cyclical process in which expected performance levels or goals are set and performance is monitored over time. It is an ongoing review of operations and activities that informs decision making and may lead to adjustments in order to meet stated goals. Evaluation is linked to the planning process. Goals are constantly reviewed and may be revised along with the activities and operations intended to accomplish them. Evaluation guides allocation and real-location of resources, a continuing activity in libraries and an integral part of the planning cycle. Much of the data required to review accomplishment of goals and to monitor programs are in the form of performance measures that focus on inputs, outputs, efficiency, effectiveness, and impact.

A technical services unit can stumble over evaluation if objectives are not clearly stated. Effective planning and unitwide understanding of the plan, goals, and objectives can help prevent this problem. Difficulties will arise if measures are uncertain, if standards or performance targets are not well formulated, or if data cannot be easily collected or verified.

Evaluation requires active monitoring and analysis. Unit heads monitor progress and implement changes in processes and activities based on what is learned. They monitor allocation and use of resources (staffing, dollars) and reallocate or request additional resources based on evaluation of data. Successful evaluation requires a systematic and coordinated system of data collection and a clear understanding of what data are needed, how they will be collected, how often they will be collected, who will collect them, who will analyze them, who will report them, who will use them, and who is empowered to act on them. Clarity on all these points is critical, and the last one is particularly important. Evaluation has little value if it does not inform decisions that improve operations and services.

Evaluation determines if a project or ongoing work is succeeding or failing. Ultimately, evaluation helps decide if a project or process or approach is worthwhile—and whether the unit will continue it or, if a project, do it again. By helping chart directions for the future, ongoing evaluation is an essential part of the planning cycle.

Summary

Evaluation is a means of improving operations and services—provided the appropriate measures are used. Typical measures consider inputs, outputs, impact, time elapsed and time expended, quality, and quantity. Technical services units typically develop their own performance standards and set performance benchmarks based on the local situation. Data can be collected manually or through automated means. A combination of measures and collection mechanisms can generate the most meaningful data. Selecting key measures that provide a balanced view of activities and progress can simplify evaluation and contributes to a balanced view of operations and activities.

Evaluation is an important tool for reporting to members of the technical services unit and to stakeholders, both within the library and outside. It documents accomplishments and demonstrates accountability. It guides requests for and allocation of resources.

Evaluation is impossible unless a library knows what it is evaluating and why. Effective evaluation is simple, repeatable, cumulative, accurate, valid, and reliable. Evaluation links planning, performance, and resource allocations. While it is critical to consider what data are collected and how, it is most important to give appropriate attention to what is done with the data and which decisions are informed by the data.

Recommended Reading

Bénaud, Claire-Lise, Sever Bordeianu, and Mary Ellen Hanson. "Cataloging Production Standards in Academic Libraries." *Technical Services Quarterly* 16, no. 3 (1999): 43–67.

Charbonneau, Michael D. "Production Benchmarks for Catalogers in Academic Libraries: Are We There Yet?" *Library Resources and Technical Services* 49, no. 1 (January 2005): 40–48.

Crawford, John. *The Culture of Evaluation in Library and Information Services.* Oxford, UK: Chandos Publishing, 2006.

Dragon, Patricia, and Lisa Sheets Barricella. "Assessment of Technical Services Workflow in an Academic Library: A Time-and-Path Study." *Technical Services Quarterly* 23, no. 4 (2006): 1–16.

Gorman, G. E., and Peter Clayton. *Qualitative Research for the Information Professional: A Practical Handbook.* 2nd ed. London: Facet, 2003.

Herrera, Gail, John Leslie, and Tina Harry. "Technical Services Serials and Monographic Ordering Assessment." *Technical Services Quarterly* 24, no. 1 (2006): 45–62.

Hiller, Steve, and James Self. "From Measurement to Management: Using Data Wisely for Planning and Decision-Making." *Library Trends* 53, no. 1 (Summer 2004): 129–55.

Johansson, David H. "An Overview of Collecting, Using, and Reporting Output Statistics in a Technical Services Department." *Public Library Quarterly* 16, no. 3 (1997): 25–40.

Smith, Glenda. "Aiming for Continuous Improvement: Performance Measurement in a Re-engineered Technical Services." *Library Collections, Acquisitions, and Technical Services* 25, no. 1 (2002): 81–91.

Notes

1. Andrew Booth, "Exceeding Expectations: Achieving Professional Excellence by Getting Research into Practice" (paper presented at LIANZA 2000 Conference, Christ Church, New Zealand, October 15–18, 2000), http://www.shef.ac.uk/scharr/elib/Exceed.pdf (accessed August 11, 2006).

2. F. W. Lancaster, *If You Want to Evaluate Your Library . . .* (Champaign: University of Illinois, Graduate School of Library and Information Science, 1988).

3. Peter Hernon and Charles R. McClure, *Evaluation and Library Decision Making* (Norwood, NJ: Ablex Publishing, 1990), 140.

4. F. W. Lancaster and Deanne McCutcheon, "Some Achievement and Limitations of Quantitative Procedures Applied to the Evaluation

of Library Services," in *Quantitative Measurement and Dynamic Library Services,* ed. Ching-chih Chen (Phoenix: Oryx Press, 1978), 12–30.

5. Thomas A. Childres and Nancy A. Van House, *What's Good? Describing Your Public Library's Effectiveness* (Chicago: American Library Association, 1993), 7.

6. Terry Hurlbert and Linda L. Dujmic, "Factors Affecting Cataloging Time: An In-House Survey," *Technical Services Quarterly* 22, no. 2 (2004): 1–14.

7. K. D. Elhard and Qiang Jin, "Shifting Focus: Assessing Cataloging Service through Focus Groups," *Library Collections, Acquisitions, and Technical Services* 28 (2004): 196–204.

8. Joe A. Hewett, "Reaction 3: Using Cost Data Judiciously," in *Cost-Effective Technical Services: How to Track, Manage, and Justify Internal Operations,* ed. Gary M. Pitkin (Chicago: American Library Association, 1989), 51.

9. Hurlbert and Dujmic, "Factors Affecting Cataloging Time."

10. Cheryl McCain and Jay Shorten, "Cataloging Efficiency and Effectiveness," *Library Resources and Technical Services* 46, no. 1 (January 2002): 23–31.

11. David C. Fowler and Janet Arcand, "A Serials Acquisitions Cost Study: Presenting a Case for Standard Serials Acquisitions Data Elements," *Library Resources and Technical Services* 49, no. 2 (April 2005): 107, 109–22; Dilys E. Morris, Collin B. Hobert, Lori Osmus, and Gregory Wool, "Cataloging Staff Costs Revisited," *Library Resources and Technical Services* 44, no. 2 (April 2000): 70–83; Dilys E. Morris and Gregory Wool, "Cataloging: Librarianship's Best Bargain," *Library Journal* 124, no. 11 (June 15, 1999): 44–46; Dilys E. Morris, Pamela A. Zager Rebarcak, and Gordon S. Rowley, "Monographs Acquisitions: Staffing Costs and the Impact of Automation," *Library Resources and Technical Services* 40 (October 1996): 301–18; Dilys E. Morris, "Staff Time and Costs for Cataloging," *Library Resources and Technical Services* 36, no. 1 (January 1992): 79–95; Lori Lynn Osmus and Dilys E. Morris, "Serials Cataloging Time and Costs: Results of an

Ongoing Study at Iowa State University," *Serials Librarian* 22, no. 1/2 (1992): 235–48.

12. Hurlbert and Dujmic, "Factors Affecting Cataloging Time."

13. American Society for Quality, Glossary, http://www.asq.org/glossary/q.html (accessed August 13, 2006).

14. Library of Congress, *Cataloging Quality: A Library of Congress Symposium* (Washington, DC: Library of Congress, 1996), 28.

15. Robert D. Stueart and Barbara B. Moran, *Library and Information Center Management,* 6th ed. (Greenwood Village, CO: Libraries Unlimited, 2002), 72.

16. Claire-Lise Bénaud, Sever Bordeianu, and Mary Ellen Hanson, "Cataloging Production Standards in Academic Libraries," *Technical Services Quarterly* 16, no. 3 (1999): 45.

17. Robert Kaplan and David Norton, *The Strategy-Focused Organization: How Balanced Scorecard Companies Thrive in the New Business Environment* (Boston: Harvard Business School Press, 2001).

CHAPTER 10

Concluding Thoughts

SOME IMPORTANT factors that contribute to a manager's success or difficulty in running a library's technical services department cannot be written in a book. These include the mix and match of personalities in the individual library, the library's history and traditions of policy and practice, the needs of various groups within the library's user population, the stage at which the library's computer systems and networking are operating, the kinds and mix of funding sources on which the library relies, and so on. The best a book can do is to describe typical situations and potential issues and problems, and suggest a range of strategies and solutions that can help address the problems and accomplish department goals.

Some elements of a manager's approach should be consistent no matter what subject or task is being discussed. These are fundamental to all the activities a manager undertakes and include the following:

- Being honest and trustworthy
- Working hard
- Keeping goals and objectives in mind
- Collaborating effectively
- Focusing on the positive and seeking win-win solutions to problems
- Doing one's job

The most effective advice sounds homely and simple: be yourself, treat others fairly, do your homework, mind your business, give credit where it is due, respect others, act ethically. But no matter how homely it may appear, such advice is well founded. It is a manager's job to motivate department staff to produce good work in sufficient quantity to meet goals and objectives, but it also is the manager's job to protect them from inappropriate assignments, unfairly low wages, physical risks, and other poor employment practices. The manager is the department's advocate in the library, not only for its share of the budget and its complement of staff but also for all the other things that make up its workplace environment. Is there no place to eat lunch or take a break? The manager should make an effort to obtain one and find an interim solution until it is available. Are the department's computers inadequately serviced? It is the manager's job to bring the problem to the attention of the appropriate people and make the case for proper maintenance. The list may be long, but the responsibility for solving the problems and creating a positive ambiance is clearly the manager's.

Managers must deal effectively with all sorts of people outside the department and the library. Among the most important of these people are the managers of other library departments, administrators who oversee the department, vendors who supply needed products and services, and peers working in other libraries. Working smoothly with all these people is merely part of the manager's job, not some special effort that goes beyond the basic call of duty. Skills (in addition to the approaches listed above) that help managers work well with everyone include communicating clearly and in a timely manner; listening to others, fulfilling promises, taking responsibility, and being concerned about the overall good of the library and the community, not solely one's own well-being or the well-being of one's department.

What professional advancement can a technical services manager expect? Career paths open to department managers include similar managerial positions in larger libraries, where they will supervise larger staffs and control larger budgets, and moving into upper-level library management, generally in their own library or one of the same size and type. Some extraordinarily successful department managers apply for and obtain directorships of large libraries, but it is more common to serve first as an assistant or associate director. Some entrepreneurial managers move from the library to the commercial world, taking positions managing operations or services in a profit-making company or going into business for themselves. A move across the line dividing not-for-profit and profit-making organizations should be made very carefully, though, because not everyone is prepared to accept all of the assumptions that underlie the world of profit.

At the end of the day, success takes more than doing the tasks listed on a manager's job description. It takes commitment to the people with whom one is involved, dedication to the services one is charged with performing, and conducting all one's business professionally. In addition, being a good manager means learning more about the job all the time—more about the materials, processes, technologies, products, and services that go into the technical services operation.

Most of all, technical services managers need to like their jobs and enjoy solving people's problems, addressing their concerns, and producing the kinds of products that enable others to succeed in doing *their* jobs, finding what they need fast, and getting what they need when and where they need it.

INDEX

Note: Page numbers in italics refer to information in text boxes.

SHEILA S. INTNER has taught technical services, library organization, and collections management since 1980. She is professor emerita in the Simmons College Graduate School of Library and Information Science and was the founding director of Simmons's MLIS program at Mount Holyoke College, established in 2001. She has taught as an adjunct professor at Catholic University of America and the University of Maryland. Over the years, Intner has consulted in collections and technical services planning, organization, and evaluation for numerous public, academic, and special libraries. In 1989, she was simultaneously elected an American Library Association Councilor-at-Large and president of the Association for Library Collections and Technical Services. She has received numerous awards, including the prestigious Margaret Mann Citation Award, the Online Audiovisual Catalogers Annual Award, and the Distinguished Alumna Award from Queens College. She is principal author/editor of twenty-two books. She holds a master's degree in Library Science from Queens College and a doctorate in Library Service from Columbia University.

PEGGY JOHNSON is associate university librarian at the University of Minnesota Libraries. She began her library career as a music cataloger and has been a children's librarian in a public library, and serials cataloger, technical services head, and a senior collection development officer in academic libraries. In 2002, she served as interim university librarian at the University of Minnesota. Johnson has consulted on library development in Uganda, Rwanda, Morocco, and China. She is a frequent speaker and consultant on collection development and management and on change in libraries, two areas of particular interest. Johnson served as president of the Association for Library Collections and Technical Services during 2000–2001. She edits the journals *Library Resources and Technical Services* (the official journal of the Association for Library Collections and Technical Services) and *Technicalities: Information Forum for the Technical Services Practitioner,* has published numerous papers, and has written and edited several books.